Ken's Greatest Challenge

MICKIE KELLY

ISBN 978-1-0980-9689-2 (paperback)
ISBN 978-1-0980-9690-8 (digital)

Christian Faith Publishing, Inc.
832 Park Avenue
Meadville, PA 16335
www.christianfaithpublishing.com

Cover photo by Jeffrey Winner

Printed in the United States of America

To the memory of Kenneth W. Kelly. It is Ken's CaringBridge diary of his battle with "the beast" for five years.

Preface

This book offers Ken's teachings, inspiring thoughts, insights, and so very much more.

There were 298 pages of encouragements and tributes from family and friends to Ken throughout this diary.

As Ken has told us many, many times, and he did just as he said, we must "carpe diem" (seize the day).

He also said, "It is what it is". But he added his own thought to this: "But it will become what you make it."

One of his closest friends said, "Your challenge is teaching me more than I would have expected. First, you teach me strength. You are letting nothing keep you down, and you still do the work of the people. Second, love of God. Third, you teach love for family and friends. And last, but certainly not least, is to carpe diem and, for that fact, to seize the moment".

This book is not about making money but about spreading Ken's inspirational message from his final physical days on earth. Any proceeds, at all, will be donated to the Hospeace House in Naples where Ken spent his last days on earth in the care of some very amazing, caring and compassionate people.

We all have learned so very much from this amazing man and will continue to pass on his legacy. Thank you, Ken, for sharing yourself with all of us!

Ken is gone, but to all of his family and friends, Ken is not gone! Carpe diem! Seize the day!

Given and presented with much love,
Mickie Kelly

Welcome to my website that I've created to keep friends and family updated about my battle with the beast "cancer". Get started by reading the introduction to the website, my story.

Background Story
(After a biopsy on April 20th, 2009)

So the doctors tell me I have prostate cancer. Worse, the cancer has spread into my bones. Now they tell me that I may have one year of relatively good health, as much as three. After that, I can expect a severe deterioration before the beast consumes me completely. I think that I've lived a life that is worthwhile. I have worked hard to leave a trail of triumph, laughter, and hope behind me. I believe in angels. I look for good in everything I see. I believe that what I receive, I must immediately give away, especially knowledge—for the good of mankind. My teaching, my work in emergency medicine is dedicated to that philosophy. I have faced many challenges in my life and career, both on the family level and in my professional life. By believing in angels and their work in the name of God, looking for good in everything I see, I have been able to meet every challenge. Now I face my greatest challenge. Even though it may take my life in the end, my philosophy has not changed. Like Job, if I keep my faith and stick by my standards, I will be able to face God, with Jesus at my side, in the end and say that I helped mankind and left a better world in my wake. My friends and my wife and family are my structure. My true friends, especially John Y. and Treff, are the pillars of my structure. In the end, I will get to walk with Jesus and see the face of God while everyone else continues to pay Caesar his due. I have met the challenge; thanks to all of you and God. I thank you for riding with me on a part of my fifty-eight-year journey. For what it's worth, it was worth all the while. I hope you had the time of your life. Thanks.

June 3rd, 2009

I had a visit with the primary doctor in charge of my case on Friday, Dr. Shapiro. What a great doctor! It was encouraging. My PSA (prostate specific antigen) has dropped a few points. The surgeon does not think that surgery is necessary at this point. (The oncologist agrees.) The prostate tumors have shrunk and the pain has, for the most part, subsided. If the hormone therapy continues to work as it is now, we won't have to do chemo or radiation right away. We'll look again at these options in four months, unless something changes before then. The cancer is in my sacrum, spine, right femur, and ribs, as well as the prostate. Aside from an annoying low back pain, I am not aware of any major discomfort. With the shrinking of the prostate tumor, I can once again sit and lie down comfortably and, best of all, ride my motorcycle. I am encouraged and optimistic. I am so grateful for the wonderful support from my friends and family. So many people have offered to assist me in any way they can by doing my chores or just being there to talk. What a wonderful life I have—what a wonderful group of human beings surround me. I am so fortunate. Despite this challenge, I have learned a lot about humanity. Thanks to all those who offer prayers in my behalf. It's working!

June 11th, 2009

It's been a tough week. The pain in my lower back is back. For the most part, I've been able to stay in front of it. Today (Thursday) is much better. I think that the classes I'm conducting are responsible for the added discomfort. I have to stand for the better part of four hours, and it's getting to me. To my extreme regret, I gave my notice to the college. I will end my full-time relationship with the Paramedic Program. It saddens me beyond belief. Teaching para-medicine has been the main focus of my professional life. I can't believe that this beast is making me give it up. I just don't want to let my students down. I don't want to be sick or unable to be in class as I struggle with the beast. Worse, I don't want to collapse in the classroom. The beast has won this little skirmish, but I'll find ways around it—maybe a recliner in the classroom and treat the lectures like a "fireside chat". Look at what FDR did in spite of his beast. I cry for my students and hope that in the end, I didn't let them or this program down. God knows best, and together, we'll get the beast!

June 16th, 2009

Tuesday—I went home last night after giving a four-hour lecture. I thought about the day and the weekend. I read all the wonderful notes left by my friends and family—my loved ones. I talked with God for a while and realized that my life is wonderful. This is just a test, and I can't let it get to me. I felt bad that I made others feel bad and worry about me. I'm really doing okay. I didn't mean to scare anyone or worry anyone. I fell into that momentary despair mode yesterday. My talk with God brought me back to reality and to the fight; I remembered that I'm not alone in it. I'm good now and ready to carry on. God has taken my despair on Himself and turned my face once again to my loved ones and their support. I feel much better, especially when I woke up from a sound sleep this morning and saw the sunshine, smelled the fresh morning air on the way to work on my bike. With all the support from everyone, how can I fail? This beast is dust, and I am happy again.

June 18, 2009

I had a preliminary evaluation yesterday. My kidneys are some-how getting involved. I have to do a follow-up with the urologist next week.

I have had so many people giving me encouragement and offering me their support. I am looking more closely at every phase of my life and how I interact with others around, including anything I say that might affect them. It's amazing how your universe can close in on you when you're told that time is shorter than you think. I found an awesome song which relates how I'm approaching life (and have been for years). It makes a lot more sense now during this battle. Here's the words—in my words.

I have a dream to help me cope with anything.
If you see the wonder of a fairy tale, you can take the
future even if you fail.
I believe in angels. I look for something good in
everything I see.
When I know the time is right for me, I'll cross the
stream.
I have a dream—a fantasy—to help me through
reality.
My destination makes it worth the while, pushing
through the darkness still another mile.
I have a dream, a song to sing to help me cope with
anything.
I believe in angels, something good in everything I
see.
When I know the time is right for me, I'll cross the
stream. I have a dream.
(adapted by me from the song by Abba, "I Have a
Dream")

The best line in this poem is the one that says, "*My destination makes it worth the while*". The day is beautiful. I have a great class tonight, Jahn has offered a chair to make my lectures easier on my back. I can't believe how everyone is digging in to make my life easier. Why couldn't I have seen all of this before now? I guess I knew, but now I can truly appreciate it. I'm truly not in this battle alone. Thank God.

June 24th, 2009

I saw the urologist. He thinks that the lymph nodes around my prostate and pelvis are the problem. He doesn't think the kidneys are affected but can't be sure. I have to go for a renal scan and ultrasound next Thursday. Some labs ahead of time and pain meds to keep the beast in the cage will get me through until the scans are done. A big thanks to Donna Spink for some extra special support and help in the paramedic school. Tad and Bill are filling for me and Heidi promises all the help I need for lectures too. God's angels are on earth—just look around you—I do. I'm feeling pretty good (physically) right now. Sleeping is hard sometimes, but Percocet is getting me through the night. The weather is glorious, my friends and family are glorious. I love life.

July 3rd, 2009

Renal scan completed last night. The radiologist will read it this morning then back to the urologist and oncologist. Pain is manageable but very distracting. Hopefully the doctors will get back to me by Monday (July 6th) after the holiday, and I am only dealing with some lymph node problem versus kidney. Jahn sent me a chair for the paramedic school. It made a difference. So many people are thinking of me. I know how blessed I am. Why does it take something like this to bring it out? Carpe diem!

July 8th, 2009

The beast got out last night and this morning—excruciating pain that took me almost three hours to get him under control again. Late for work, but the beast in my pelvis is finally back in the cage. I have to stay in front of the pain. I'm afraid that the meds are messing with my brain. I can't remember words and sometimes my thoughts are really jumbled. I have to stop and think about how to say things that normally I could just spin out. Just keep battling, I can control this. Thanks for listening. It's getting better.

July 10th, 2009

Good news from the urologist this evening: The kidney scan is negative—no cancer in the kidneys! There is some swelling; it is from the lymph nodes. Pain is bone pain. He upped the pain meds and I have to see the oncologist next week. I am so relieved. Half this battle is knowing where you stand. God has answered me and He is good and glorious. I thank Him for all of my friends and family for supporting me. We will beat this beast into submission!

July 17th, 2009

It's been a great week. The pain is well under control and I've slept reasonably well. I actually feel good, healthy. Each day that I feel good is a gift. I pray and hope for many more to come. Thanks for thinking of me this week. Your prayers are working.

July 21st, 2009

It was a good week all last week—very little pain, and I slept well. The low back pain and flank pain are back today. I spent a restless night. (Ask Poko—and I found my pillows all over the room when I woke up.) Percocet has the beast locked up though—I'm doing okay. I Have another kidney test on Thursday morning. The urologist is talking about a stent. I had several visitors last weekend. I love visitors. What a great weekend. Carpe diem!

July 30th, 2009

Today's visit to the oncologist (Dr. Yirinec who I really like) produces a mixture of news—good and bad. The good news is that the kidneys are still clear of disease. The unsettling news is that this very aggressive, high-grade cancer has spread from my left sacrum into my right sacrum and right femur. The flank pain appears to be coming from the sacrum and lower spinal vertebrae. He has scheduled me for a pelvic scan next week in an effort to clarify just what's going on. It appears the next step, depending on the pelvic scan, will be to begin infusing of Zoledronic Acid IV, which will lead to some very unpleasant side effects. If it holds the beast in check, then I am willing to do battle and stand my ground despite the discomfort it will cause. I just hope that I can continue to work and teach effectively—I owe it to my colleagues and especially to my students. I pray and know that God will stand before me as we begin the battle. Carpe diem!

August 4th, 2009

Very good news from Dr. Yirinec today: The PSA and blood-work numbers are looking good. I have a pelvic scan next week to see where the beast lies asleep. We are trying some strong but conservative meds to control pain. It looks like the hormone therapy has the beast in check—so no chemo right now. Thank God. We are on top of things and I'm on top of the world. Carpe diem!

August 11th, 2009

Got a little behind it this weekend—I'm catching up now and feeling pretty good. I start a new med this week because of extreme weakness in my right leg. New med is to help with bone density. It might make me a little sick, agitated, etc. I can handle that without a problem. The nice weather helps too, as well as several opportunities to be with family and friends, picnics, a BBQ, and such. Lecturing is getting harder. I have trouble standing all that time, even with the chairs, it's tough. I have about a three-week break in classes. That will help. Carpe diem!

August 13th, 2009

I still haven't caught up. I'm not in front of the pain yet. It's been a tough, tough week. My legs are giving out more and more and the pain is a constant companion. I almost passed out at the meeting last night. I got up five times during the night. I am so tired. I stood in the shower this morning and wept. I know that's not being strong, but it was a private place. It wasn't so much the pain as the job ahead. There is so much I want to see and do. I want to see my students graduate. I want to build and see my new five- and ten-year business plans go forth at Finger Lakes Ambulance. I want to see Dylan graduate. I want to see John Y. and Lisa happy again. I want to witness all of my nieces and nephews grow up, graduate and get married. I weep because I realize that I may not and that's selfish and only considering me. I talked with God while I stood in that shower. I know it's not going to be easy. I remembered Job and how he remained faithful through all the tribulations that he suffered. I will not let my family, my colleagues, my students, or my friends down. After I talked with God, I remembered that my destination would make it all worthwhile. I was so happy last night after a meeting with the college staff. They have now appointed some of the best minds and certainly the most incredible paramedics—paramedic instructors in the state—to take my place. Now that the appointments are made, I am at ease, knowing that my students and this program, that I have given my heart to, are in the very best of hands. I'm sorry I cried this morning. I'll be fine. It is only here that I will admit it and only here, where my true friends seek me out, that I would tell of my anguish. Thanks for listening and for understanding. Tomorrow we try a new med. I will get in front again. I won't cry again. God awaits me and it will be in His time, not mine. Amen.

August 19th, 2009

What a difference a few days and some new meds make! I feel so good—better than I have in a month. Thanks to everyone who propped me up last week and weekend. You'll never know how much it helps and how much safer it makes me feel. I hope these meds keep working for forever 'cause I am so renewed.

August 29th, 2009

It's Saturday. The three treatments are done. I feel better than I have in months. I was a little sick each time, but it only lasted a day. The pain is much diminished and I am sleeping well. Each day is a blessing—each good day, a gift. Thank God, and thank You, God, for my friends and loved ones. With God before me and all my friends and family standing with me, how can I fail? I feel so good. I am overjoyed.

September 3rd, 2009

I have mixed news today from the doctor. I am feeling pretty good other that the constant back and flank pain. He is not sure exactly what is causing it. We are scheduling an MRI and another bone scan to see if they can find anything treatable. I will get another round of chemicals (medications?) perhaps next week after the tests and another Lupron on October 2nd. I am now anemic with a low hematocrit, which we'll treat with vitamins. My RBCs (red blood cell count) are larger than normal—the hematologist will figure that out. I will see a neurologist next week to help with the lower back pain and flank pain. It's getting to be pretty routine. I am in good spirits and feel like we're on top of this thing. It's amazing how this thing can alter body systems and functions. Of course the chemicals can change lots. At least I'm not sick from the chemicals (not much anyhow). Just staying in front of the pain is a great achievement. Hangin' in there!

September 9th, 2009

The beast is on the prowl. He struggled hard the last twenty-four hours, sending me to an emergent appointment with the doctor this morning. The Rx (prescription) is ongoing Percocet, Lupron Rx, Cortisone, and Bicalutamide. I'm still in control, still in front. Now I need a cane to keep from falling over—weakness in my right leg. Coming up are MRI and bone scan to try and locate the source of the trouble. I know the source, it's the beast. If they can pinpoint his whereabouts, we'll nail him with some radiation. I'm okay with everything. It's a bit inconvenient, and the beast seethes under the Percocet cloud; but I'm out here, and he's tied up in there. I know my destination, so it makes it all worthwhile. Carpe diem!

September 11th, 2009

I don't know why, but I feel so much better today. No doubt, the Oxycodone has a lot to do with it. My back pain is diminished today, and I just feel good. I am walking better, although the leg weakness makes me a little unsteady, but it doesn't hurt! Whatever it is, I sure hope it keeps going for lots of days. The beast is sleeping. Good days build my strength and resolve so that I am prepared when the beast stirs about. I just feel great.

September 29th, 2009

It's been a couple of good weeks—this one, not so much. The pain is not so bad as it has been—under control for the most part. The legs are in abandon mode. All of a sudden, they just aren't under me when I'm walking along. I see the neurologist this week. Hopefully we'll find the problem and get walking again without fear of falling. I'm a little depressed today, this week, I'm sorry to say. Sometimes I just can't help it. I'm working hard to keep upbeat and stay strong. My friends and family are so much help in that respect, I don't want to disappoint them. Sometimes I just feel like I want to lay back and close my eyes, maybe forever, hoping it will all go away. The constant ache makes it hard, it's there even when I lie still. Have you ever asked why bad things happen to you? I have this week. I'm walking with Jesus, and I'm afraid that I'm squeezing His hand a little too hard this week. Just knowing that I have His hand helps. I hope this doesn't sound too dark. Chemicals this Friday. Maybe I'll see the brighter side of things afterward. Thanks for listening to me, for being there.

October 3rd, 2009

I had appointments with my attending, the urologist, the neurologist, the insurance company, and the lab(s) yesterday. I had a neuromuscular function test, which was painful and left me very uncomfortable. I now have even more pills to take. It has been a dark week for me. I struggle daily to keep from crying, but it has given me time to reflect on a lot of things. I am selfish for dwelling in the darkness that has overcome me because I have so many things to be grateful for. I ask God's understanding and forgiveness for my weakness in this black fog that I am in because I know that His Son is standing right beside me the whole time.

I have read, and I have come to realize that I would never trade my amazing friends, my wonderful life, my loving family for less gray hair or a flatter belly or even a longer life for myself. As I work through this challenge, I've become kinder to myself and less critical of myself. I've become my own friend. I don't chide myself for eating that extra cookie or for not making my bed or for buying those silly plastic lions that I didn't need but looks so avant-garde on my front porch. I am entitled to a cookie, to be messy, to be extravagant.

I have seen too many leave this world too soon before they understood the great freedom that comes with a full life. Whose business is it if I choose to read or play on the computer until 4:00 a.m. and sleep until noon? I will sing as loud as I can in my car to those wonderful tunes of the sixties and seventies, and if I, at the same time, wish to weep over the anguish of my best friends as they suffer discord in their lives, I will.

I will walk the beach in a swimsuit that is stretched over a bulging body and will dive into the waves with abandon if I choose to, despite the pitying glances from the jet set.

I know I am sometimes forgetful. But there again, some of life is just as well forgotten. And I eventually remember the important things.

Sure, over the years, my heart has been broken. How can your heart not break when you lose a cherished relationship, when your best friends cannot find a common course to repair a broken relationship, when a child suffers, or even when somebody's beloved pet gets hit by a car? But broken hearts are what give us strength and understanding and compassion. A heart never broken is pristine and sterile and will never know the joy of being imperfect.

I am so blessed to have lived long enough to have my hair turn gray and to have my youthful laughs be forever etched into deep grooves on my face. So many have never laughed, and so many have died before their hair could turn silver. As you get older, it is easier to be positive. You care less about what other people think. I don't question myself anymore. I've even earned the right to be wrong. So I like living. It has set me free. I like the person I have become. I am not going to live forever, but while I am still here, I will not waste time lamenting what could have been or worrying about what will be. And I shall eat cookies every single day (if I feel like it).

If you are reading this, if you are here in my private place of comfort, thanks for being here for me. May our hearts never come apart. Thank God for allowing me to approach the end of my life knowing the deep love of friendship and family and of having you in my life. One of God's greatest blessings upon me is that I have been allowed to have given and received friendship, knowledge and love and knowing that I hate no one on this earth.

October 19th, 2009

The beast has tentacles, and he is insidious. I had a contrast scan of my kidneys today and an MRI of my spine. The pain is under control. We will seek out the beast.

What a wonderful weekend I had. I attended an awards banquet in which my peers saw fit to offer me recognition for my work. NYS Department of Health gave me the Educator of Excellence award and made me the Educator of the Year—all for just doing what I love to do. I look for good in everything I see. When I find it, I grow it! Soon all the good I've grown serves to make this world a better place for all. I am humbled and honored at the same time. The weekend with my colleagues, friends, and family made me forget all about the beast.

Wednesday we find the results of the scan and MRI. I will pray for the best and that God guides my physicians in pursuit of the beast and his defeat—if not for me in my time, then for those that follow me and struggle also with this monster called cancer. Carpe diem!

October 21st, 2009

The MRI from Monday brings sad and scary news. This cancer has spread into my lumbar vertebrae. It is the tentacles of the beast as he reaches out, invading wherever he can. The tumors on my spine and sacrum are what is most likely causing both pain and weakness. We'll continue the pain meds along with the chemicals that I am already being treated with. Now we will do a lumbar puncture to look in the CSF (cerebrospinal fluid) for cancer cells. We are in hopes that the tumors do not invade the spinal cord. All told, I'm doing okay. The pain is under control. Knowing what is going on makes me feel better. I know the beast. Not knowing what he is doing is what is scary. Now that I know, I am stronger for it.

God knows where He wants me to go and when He wants me to arrive. I know what my destination is. I rely upon Him and will go where He leads me. He gives me only what I can handle, and there is purpose in this challenge.

November 6th, 2009

It's been a good week, better than most. The chemicals are helping—once a month now.

I have been giving a lot of thought to my present today, as well as my future. I reviewed a couple of ambulance calls this week, both suicides. I don't know the reason for the first. I do know that the second had numerous health problems and had told his friends and family that if his health worsened then he didn't want to live like that. He ended his life. I anguish for him as well as the first person, yet I somehow understand them. Sometimes quantity is not as important as quality. It even seems as though it could be the right thing to do at times.

I could not and would not do such a thing to my family and friends who are fighting as hard as I am to control the beast. I feel sad that these two people may not have had the wonderful experience of my family and friends. My body gives me almost constant pain. The weakness that follows me step-by-step reminds me of how hard

I must work to finish the journey assigned to me. Until I come to the end, I will rely upon my faith and my exceptional friends and ever-loving family to prove to the beast that we can make a difference. I will not allow this battle to be finished until I have been given every minute possible to discover the beast and subdue it.

If I can live long enough, perhaps the physicians and scientists can learn enough about my beast to discover new ways to control and even destroy him. Maybe it won't be in time to extend my life. If my battle can produce steps toward saving another human being, then the pain and weakness that I must bear are a gift from God and not the burden it appears to be to others who watch my battle. The gift from God that comes from my battle might just well be a longer and healthier life for another person. What a great gift for me to know that my battle had turned into a gift of life to them.

I will not travel the path that the two poor souls did this week. The precious gift of life given to me by God is not mine to keep and I will need it to exchange for the life that Jesus has promised me in my forever future. I wish I could have talked with these poor people before they carried out their plan. Maybe they just didn't know. We must strive every day to leave this earth and those that dwell upon it in a better condition than we found it. It is the task that God has given us.

Thank you for your love. Thank you for your friendship. Thank you for being here when I need you.

November 17th, 2009

Another good week has gone by. I am feeling pretty good. We're making adjustments in the many medications I am taking, and that seems to be helping me physically, joyfully and mentally. My outlook has improved.

My darling cousin Jahn sent my wife and I each a crazy pair of socks—mismatched and a wild color combination—what great fun! We sneaked them on as part of our uniform at work just because we felt like we were getting away with something. (And we did!) We need to do some crazy things now and again. It reminds us of the beauty of life, and despite our concerns—bills and ills—we can still have fun enjoying simple things. Thank you, Jahn, for making some of our time here sunnier, happier, and memorable.

I have another round of chemicals this week. The beast is seeking sanctuary from their effects and hides his ugly head for now. My pain is much subdued, and with great care in walking, the weakness in my legs is tolerable. Maybe the holidays will be full of fun things, like crazy colored, mismatched socks, and maybe the beast will sleep through these special days and allow me the time at peace with my family and with my friends. Sunshine is everywhere if you take the time to look for it.

November 19th, 2009

I have to have some chemicals today (Friday) to keep the beast sleeping. They have to increase the dose and the results promise to provide hours of discomfort, maybe misery. I am not going to hide the truth—I'm a little scared. Army sergeants, good educators, the boss—they're not supposed to be scared, are they? I decided that if I thought about fun things—things I love—and that if I keep thinking about them, that the next couple of days would be easier for me. These are things that make me happy.

- Mickie
- When Poko jumps around because he is happy to see me
- Chocolate chip cookies
- Macaroni and cheese
- Photographs
- Eating a large baked potato with plenty of salt and butter
- Having a student thank me for having given them understanding
- Buying gifts for people I love
- When the thunder is so loud it makes the windows rattle
- Taking off my shoes and my shirt
- Singing at the top of my lungs while driving (You really have to ride with me to appreciate this one!)

- The smell of coffee when my brother opens a new can
- Looking at photos of my mother and father, grandmother and grandfather, aunts and uncles, and brothers and knowing that I have a part of all of these wonderfully diverse people in me
- Relaxing by candlelight with a nice glass of wine, listening to music I love
- A great idea
- Eating a spoon of peanut butter
- Watching people caring about their friends
- A big hug from my best friend's five-year-old son
- Letting my nieces and nephews play in my hair
- The aroma of a BBQ
- Going to bed on sheets that have been hanging on a clothesline in the sunshine all day
- Country music, a six pack, and some friends
- To see a child filled with joy for any reason—a child's laughter
- Clean teeth
- Walking into a room and many people call out my name in greeting
- Having a good laugh with friends
- Knowing that there is someone who would do anything for me
- Riding through the countryside on my motorcycle and smelling all the different smells and feeling the temperature changes too
- Lisa's special oyster crackers
- Walking with Jesus and talking with God
- The feeling I get sometimes where just being alive on this beautiful planet is all I could ask for
- My best friend
- And most of all—needing a hug on my chemo day and then finally getting one from a best friend and my loved ones

Thank you for coming to my place of comfort today because you just made this day easier for me.

November 27th, 2009

Last weekend was brutal. Things got a little better as each day of this week went by. I think I'm beginning to get accustomed to the chemicals, or maybe the half-life is getting shorter. I feel good today and look forward to three reasonably good weeks before we do it all over again.

I was talking to a young man this morning who received a preliminary diagnosis from his doctors related to some headaches he was having and a possibility that he may have a beast on board. We talked for quite a while. I hope that I was able to help him to understand the nature of the beast and to rely on love, faith, friends, and family in order to face the battle ahead.

After he left, I got to thinking about the "time" that the doctors are talking about. I started to deliberate on what that really meant to me. My doctors told me that I most likely would have a year of reasonably good health and, with luck, as much as three before this beast consumes me. After talking to the young man this morning, I needed to put this "time" thing into perspective. I have an awful lot to do today at work; the papers were piled high on my desk. I also wanted to make a couple of calls to a friend in another state and touch base with my best friend who is going through some pretty rough times himself. Being a good manager, I had to set my priorities; but the "time" thing kept nudging me as I set about trimming the size of the paper pile. After a few minutes of nagging (from my conscience?), I stopped to try a little experiment.

I set my watch alarm for one hour. I said to myself, "This is all the time you have, one hour." I worked furiously at the paper pile after I set the alarm. I kept looking at the clock. I didn't have to take my blood pressure or pulse; I know it was going up as the seconds ticked by. I was almost in a dead panic when the last few seconds trickled through the little electronic timekeeper. The alarm went off. Not only did I not finish the paper pile, but worse than that, I didn't get to call my buddy out of state or talk with my best friend to offer him encouragement and support. My time had run out.

It kind of puts things in perspective, doesn't it? I reset my alarm clock today. It's set for one year, and that's all the time I have. I now know my priorities. I will take care of my friends and my family, my students, my employees, and myself. As far as the paper pile, I have an obligation to finish that as well, but I can delegate that because now, for less than a year, I have priorities (because the clock started ticking already). If the alarm goes off in a year and I'm still here, then God has blessed me. Then I will thank my God, reset the alarm and my priorities.

Say "I love you" to someone that you do. Give a hug, male or female, because it's not a sexual thing but a human thing. Put your arm around your best friend, and support him or her, knowing that your troubles aren't the only ones in the universe. Don't put that stuff off because the time to get it all done is gone too soon.

This is my private place. I can say just how I am feeling and what my deepest thoughts are. I welcome you and am pleased that you care enough about me and about humanity to visit here when I'm often at my worst. You make me better, and it means the world to me. Thank you.

December 10th, 2009

I spoke with the oncologist about an hour ago. They have found spots on my spinal cord. I am more scared today than I have ever been in my whole life. I'm not scared of my destination or the end of my journey, for Jesus said that He has prepared a room for me in His Father's mansion. I am scared of the journey itself.

Please forgive me for my weakness. The news caught me off guard. I know that I will remain upright on this journey. How can I not with my friends and family and those who love me so closely surrounding me? I pray for the strength to remain strong and faithful as we begin the next battle with this beast.

I will be leaving for a long weekend in Florida tomorrow. I will see the oncologist next week for a follow-up. I want to just relax and not think too much about this new change. I am scared. I hope you understand this weak moment. Thank you for being here for me if you are here now. My journey will be easier.

December 16th, 2009

In a moment of weakness last week, I admitted to you that I was scared. That was true, I was scared. The weakness was in forgetting God. I went to Florida for a few days. I had dinner with my wife and some very, very dear friends. I sat on the beach and watched as heaven and earth came together on the horizon. I had time on that quiet beach to hold the hand of my Lord Jesus, and we talked to God.

I had become scared, and in my fear, I had forgotten the promise: He answered, "Love the Lord God with all your heart and with all your soul and with all your strength and with all your mind. Do this, and you will live."

I knew that this meant *all* my faith, not just a part of me. I must love my fellow man as I love myself and keep giving my time, efforts, life, and love to make this wonderful earth a better place for everyone. If I give up on myself, I give up on the mission God has set forth for me, which is mankind—my family, my friends, my coworkers, my students, and those that hurt just like me. I know that I will live after the end of my journey. I know this with *all* of my heart, soul, strength, and mind.

I saw the oncologist today and will have a follow-up on Friday. My mission isn't done. My being scared is gone. Let the battle begin.

December 30th, 2009

My visit with the oncologist today brought good news and some new plans. The spots on my spine are all but gone! My PSA is 0.5. (I started this journey at 38!) We are to try a new chemical infusion next Thursday. The goal is to eliminate the chronic and persistent pain. The treatment will be once a month for three months.

I am enthused. We have a good plan. You can't be scared all the time. Eleanor Roosevelt once said, "*You gain strength, courage and confidence by every experience in which you really stop to look fear in the face*".

This battle with the beast has taught me that you must do the thing that you think you cannot do. You must stop and face the fear nose to nose, eye to eye. It gives me courage to do that—to face fear. With courage, you will dare to take risks, have the strength to be compassionate and the wisdom to be humble. Courage is the foundation of integrity. Courage is not the absence of fear but rather the judgment that something else is more important than fear. That something else is life, love, family, friends, and faith. I want you to know that your visit today means more to me than anything else in this world. As long as I have you with me, dearest of readers, dearest friend, then I have no fear, and I find that I do have courage to do this thing in the end.

January 11th, 2009

Today I have returned from three days of incredible physical pain and discomfort. I took chemotherapy last Thursday, the new chemical attack on the beast. It knocked me off my feet.

Confucius once wrote, "*Our greatest glory is not in never falling but in rising every time we fall*". I kept telling myself over these last few days that I will rise, this thing *will not* keep me down. Today, Monday, I am much recovered and willing to take on this beast no matter how many times it causes me to fall. Someday soon, a bright medical mind will discover a simple "gene switch" in our DNA that can turn cancer off. One little injection of this switch into the bloodstream will shut down the beast from the start, and we can stop using howitzers to shoot at fleas. Maybe it won't be in my time. Maybe by me taking these howitzer shots, it will help bring that brilliant scientist closer to finding that simple switch that will help someone else avoid this agony. Each time I rise, it gives us one more shot at this beast to learn its secrets.

I am much better today. I was able to eat again and keep it down. Physically, I feel okay. What a glorious day for me and for the rest of the world because we are all living. If you and I, and maybe lots of other people, would only stop and look at the sunshine and know that some little thing that each one of us could do for someone else could make life a little better for that person, then the world would be a better place to be in. Isn't that the glory we are searching for?

Thank you for taking time to visit me here when I am at my worst. You give me cause to rise each time, and I will.

January 28th, 2010

I am looking forward to my next round of chemicals next week with a bit of apprehension given my body's reaction the last time. I am not in fear nor dread, but unpleasant things are just that— unpleasant and typically not to be enjoyed or looked forward to.

This battle that I am engaged in has taken me from stoic pragmatism to being a reflective pragmatist (if there is such a being). When you are faced with what is truly the battle of your life, you stop and think about a lot of things. In my case, it's not what might have been, nor a wish to change much about my life because I'm pretty happy about how I've lived my life. I don't have many regrets. I'm not angry that I may not live to be one hundred, something that I always took for granted would happen, and I'm not angry. As a matter of fact, the experts have told me I may not make it to sixty. Quite frankly I'm not angry about anything at all. I do know that I now cherish the life that I have, and I am far more aware of my life as time slips away. I am very aware of what I am doing each minute, knowing that my minutes are now limited.

Muhammed Ali said, "*Don't count the days, but instead make the days count*". So that's what I've learned to do, that's what this beast has taught me. I don't waste time in the past nor give a lot of my allotted time to dreaming or worrying about what might be in the future. I am enjoying my life and my relationships day by day, minute by minute, and I cherish each and every second of my life. In the end, I want to be able to say that I've enjoyed every single hour, minute, second that was given to me. I want to be able to say that I made life count, love count, friendships count and had joy all the way to the end.

So I'm not worried about the next chemo treatment or the next or the one after that. I don't like it, but by taking it, it gives me an extra hour, minute, second with my loved ones and you, my friend, living and loving life. Carpe diem!

February 4th, 2010

I laid in bed last night; little Poko laid quietly next to me. He was breathing a little hard, some crackles in his lungs. He is eleven now, and I fear he has some congestive heart failure. I petted him. I said, "It's okay, little Poko. We are both dying together". Then I cried.

Chemo is today. I spoke with God this morning while on the way to work in my car. I asked Him to take this bitter plate from my table. There was total silence; even the emergency radios in my car became quiet. I realized that I was wrong in asking this. It should not be my will but His, for God is always right and there is a purpose in all of this. It's not about my struggle but what my struggle will mean to a better understanding of the beast inside. It's for a healthier and kinder world.

I'm leaving for chemo. I am so thankful for you, my friends, coming here today. I can bear this with you by my side. Please pray for me. Please.

February 7th, 2010

I was so depressed, so full of apprehension on Thursday, when I wrote in this journal. I just wanted to run as far away as I could and try and forget this awful thing. I am so much better today. I'm sorry if I caused you to fear and worry from my last journal entry. Just knowing that you are here gives me the strength because I know that I'm not alone. It is a year now since we found the beast within. We are in front and I vow the next twenty years will find us still strong in the faith that this will be overcome.

I came out of the darkness this weekend after my treatment stronger and more reassured. The doctors gave me medicines to ease the side effects. It made all the difference. Today I feel healthy, my pain is so much subdued. My spirits are high. I greet this day with faith, strong in my heart. I will love the sun because it warms me; yet I love the rain and the snow because it cleanses my spirit. I love the light, for it shows me the way; yet I understand the darkness because it shows me the stars and how far we can reach if we desire. I welcome happiness because it gives me peace; yet I can endure this dark struggle because it opens my soul and renews my faith.

I promise to acknowledge happiness when it comes my way; yet I welcome obstacles for they are my challenge and make me stronger. When my time does come and my friends and loved one's gaze upon my tombstone and see the two dates—one, the beginning of my journey through this life and the other the end—I hope that they will only remember the dash between the dates. I hope that they will think of the light and dark, the happiness and occasional sadness, the faith and hope, and that the dash represents my true desire to have left mankind better off than when I arrived and that I achieved some measure of success in that mission.

Thank you, dearest friend, for coming here today.

February 23rd, 2010

Today, dear journal reader, I won't subject you to my philosophy of life nor my dark feelings about this beast that I battle because the oncologist has given me hope with some happy progress information.

My most recent scan shows no new lesions in my bones. In fact we are showing shrinking of some of the existing tumors, especially in my prostate. The oncologist refused to utter the word remission. I can accept that. My flank pain is completely gone, my low back pain is minor and intermittent. My hip gives me some pain, but my legs have regained their strength, and I don't feel as though they aren't under me when I walk anymore. I can finally sleep through the night.

My dearest cousin Jahn would advise me to run outside and jump for joy. I'm not ready to express myself to that extent, but believe me, my heart and soul are bouncing madly about in happiness. For the first time, I feel as though we have the upper hand.

The doctor tells me that I must continue the chemo treatments, once each month and an injection every so often. Despite the physical discomfort that comes with those treatments, I can now see that they are working. I feel better now than I have in eighteen months.

I hope that this happy news gives you a portion of the joy that I feel today. I am so glad that you are here to share it with me. It's good to write in this journal without despair. It's good to be here today.

March 5th, 2010

Chemo yesterday and here I am today, still alive and still fighting! Abe Lincoln once wrote during the darkest days of the fight for the Union's preservation, *"I may walk slowly, but I never walk backward"*. So here I go again, one foot in front of the other, never looking back and never walking backward. Me and my doctors, we're in front, and in front we will stay, God by our sides.

I vowed the challenge wouldn't leave me lost in the black cloud anymore and it won't. I woke to brilliant sunshine this morning, the day after, and I will exist in that sunshine today and forevermore.

Did you ever get inspired by something someone else wrote or said? I am a voracious reader. I usually have three or four books going at once, not including my science and medical journals. I like to think that I am a good observer and an excellent listener. I love to hear other's observations and ideas. I guess that leaves me as an imitator and not a great or original thinker. If I learn from someone else and pass it along, does it count? If it helps someone else to see, to appreciate, to be thankful for their own blessings despite their woes? I know it makes me happier and stronger to hear great quotes and great ideas and to take inspiration from them. Here's one from Tolkien that inspires me in some of my dark times (like chemo day):

All that is gold does not glitter, not all those who wander are lost. The old that is strong does not wither, deep roots are not reached by the frost. From the ashes a fire shall be woken, a light from the

shadows shall spring. Renewed shall be blade that
was broken. The crownless again shall be king.

How can you not take hope and inspiration from a guy like him? Carpe diem!

March 15th, 2010

Just when you think things are okay, the beast takes another bite. Or should I say, it lays there gnawing on me. The pain just won't go away.

The good news is there's no new fractures. That good news doesn't explain the return of the pain in my lower back. It went away for a while but now comes creeping back. It prevents me from sleeping. I am just so tired. I don't dare take any more medication, or I won't be able to function. I don't want to keep going back and complaining about pain to the doctors. I know there's pain associated with the beast, and I don't want to seem like a whiner. God, if I only had a day to rest with no pain. Dear God, please just let me sleep.

March 16th, 2010

I just got back from the oncologist. It appears the cancer has migrated to my left hip. An MRI is to confirm his suspicions. I'm off work for a couple of days until the results come in. X-rays today show that my lower spinal vertebrae have degenerated and are most likely the cause of my deepening pain. Today I started around the clock morphine. After the MRI results, Dr. Yirinec thinks that we will need radiation to get back in front of this awful beast.

Right now, and more than anything else, I just wish I could have a hug from someone.

March 28th, 2010

The beast makes itself known mostly by pain now. Morphine finally gives me peace at night, and I'm able to sleep, and Morphine by day allows me to continue to work. My PSA is very low, and the beast, normally detected by PSA levels, hides. Because of the low PSA but unremitting pain, we have sought out the beast and find that he has changed his coat!

I had an appointment and physical from the radiation oncologist on Friday. I learned from Dr. Hansen that the beast has "cloned" himself. Prostate cancer cells, even those that migrate to other places, such as my bones, continue to give off prostate specific antigen (PSA), a marker of the beast's presence. Now the beast had produced clone cancer cells which are cancer cells that do not emit PSA. The beast (cancer) can now go undetected except for one thing: Wherever he goes, he is destructive, and the result is pain. It accounts for the unremitting pain that I have had despite a good PSA. A CT scan on Monday will pinpoint the beast in his various hiding places. Drs. Hansen and Yirinec have agreed that the clone cancer cells can be best dealt with using radiation. I will take daily radiation for the next four weeks along with the infusions and injections.

This pain, this pursuit of the beast, has occupied my mind almost constantly. It makes it very tough to concentrate on my daily work. Last week was a difficult week at work. There were many, many issues. I did my best to focus on taking care of those issues to make sure the excellent people that work for me and who I work with are taken care of. I fear the beast is so distracting me that I haven't given my friends and staff the attention they deserve. I am hoping that the radiation will put this beast off and let me take care of those that depend upon me. What an evil beast this is. It has no regard for the needs of humanity. I will do my best to do my job until I can't any longer, but I will not let this go on so long that I falter and lose the confidence of staff.

I am buoyed by you and am grateful that you have come here today. I am upheld by your presence here, by your support, by your love. God is with me in this. With God leading me and with you, my friends, my family, and Jesus by my side, how can we fail? Thank you.

March 30th, 2010

I went in for the first of my radiation sessions yesterday. Strange, the things you think of while lying on a table with modern medical technology making odd sounds all around you. I was thinking about how many more times I would be doing this, shoving this poor body through these humming machines, watching poison drip into my veins. Sometimes you wonder why you do it, put up with it. Why do I keep pushing and hoping for what seems impossible? Will I be cured? Will I be a wiser, better man for it? More importantly, how is all of this going to help someone else? I remember something I read in the past; John Ruskin's comment one hundred years ago is fitting to answer my questions: "*The highest reward for man's toil is not what he gets for it, but what he becomes by it*".

I finally found an oncologist who smiles and even jokes with me. Most do not, and I can't blame them. They are dealing with the seemingly impossible, and most often it winds up in death. When I was told that because of the widespread metastasis of this cancer that it would inevitably be terminal, my question was "How terminal is it?" Life is terminal. I don't know a single person alive today who was here in the beginning. What's important is that it's not a matter of when I will face death but what I do in the meantime. I am not afraid of death. I believe in angels and their work for the good of man in God's name. Of course the struggle is worth it; for what it's worth, it was worth all the while. I am happy.

The happiness of life is made up of minute fractions, the little soon forgotten charities of a true and well-meant hug, a smile, a kind look, a heartfelt compliment in the disguise of a playful raillery, and the countless other infinitesimals of pleasurable thought and genial feeling.

The happiness I feel isn't any one thing. It's a multiple of minute fractions—my wife's kiss as she meets me by the door, Poko's excited dancing about as he waits for me to pick him up and hug him. My house is warm. My emails are full of encouragement and words of faith and friendship. My belly is full. My bed is clean, soft and warm. My staff smiled all day at work. The pharmacist at Wegman's went out of her way to help me understand how the new cancer medication will work and then clasped my hand in such a caring way that I knew she shared my pain in this struggle. I thought of all the nice things people did and said all day long. How could anyone not be happy when there is so much nice about—more nice than not nice? There are three essential things in my life that are simple but led strength to living: love, search to knowledge, and an unbearable need to help alleviate the suffering of mankind. Renounce hate—don't let it enter your life at all. Imagine all the room it would leave for love and for caring and the time to help someone else. As my treatment ended, and I prepared to climb off that table, I thought, some people walk in the rain, others just get wet. I am in the rain, and I know it. As my knowledge grows, my fears decrease. With increased knowledge, we think less of worshipping the unknown and more of overcoming it. I'm no fool. I know my life will end and that I can be replaced in all the things that I do on this earth. The graveyards are full of irreplaceable people. I like to think that I walk in the rain, that I'm not just getting wet.

Have faith in what God has promised. Declare hate dead in your heart and mean it. Live every single moment as if it were your last, but plan for forever. I love life.

April 19th, 2010

I'm kind of down today, so please forgive me a moment of weakness. I know tomorrow will be better. For the last two weeks, I have undergone radiation treatments daily. While generally painless, I have found unpleasant side effects, which are affecting my spirits no matter how hard I work to keep them up. After two weeks of steady bombardment, the treatments have drained me of energy. GI upset has been pretty constant, something that I've been trying to control by diet. Food of almost any kind makes me nauseous, sometimes just the thought of it. The deep bone pain is being controlled by round-the-clock Morphine, which has its own side effects. It's been a pretty miserable weekend. As you can see, this round of treatment has been a bit tough and it's got me a little down.

Generally, I keep my spirits up because of the encouragement you give me. I don't know how I could cope with this but for my friends and loved ones who support me daily and demonstrate caring and love by visits or kind words here in my journal or personally. I am blessed to know you. I am blessed to have so many who care so deeply. I know that what lies behind me and what I have yet to face depend a great deal upon how I handle today, this moment. Thank God that I have angels like you whose strong wings keep me up. Thank you.

April 29th, 2010

I finished my four-week course of radiation this week. I have a month off and then back for an evaluation. It has been brutal this last week. The break from daily radiation will make things get slowly better. Today is chemo, so tonight will likely be a night to lie low so that I can function tomorrow. The weather guys are promising sun and warmth for the weekend—for me, a new start.

I love life, sun, my friends, and my family. I got to thinking about that as time for the chemo gets closer and I prepare for the evil side effects—how my family has grown even as it shrinks. What is family anyhow? It's more that kindred blood in my veins. It's the people that I am with every single day. It turns out to be my family, my friends, and my coworkers. It is the people that I interact with every single day. They are my everything. They are what make this life so worth the while.

I thought about when my mom and dad died several years apart. I cried on both occasions as the realization struck that they had slipped from my grasp and that I was never ever going to be able to hug or kiss them again. I wasn't even going to be able to tell them one last time that I loved them or ask for their forgiveness for saying things over the years, in angry times, that I really and truly didn't mean. I felt so empty, so helpless. It was painful learning that sometimes there isn't any more time. What we love, what we care about, is just not there and never will be there again—gone in a flash. And there was nothing I could do to change it. It is so final.

I guess that that's what this is about today. "I love life" is such an important statement. As tough as things are, as poorly as I feel, at least I have life now. At least I have friends now. At least I have love for that which I have and those that care so much about me. These are things that make life valuable—things that are special, people that are special, moments in time that are fleeting. These are the things that make it all worth the while. So now I must cherish it before that painful moment comes, as it will, and it all goes away. When I was a young man, I had thousands of days ahead of me—now maybe not so many. So now I am compelled to seize the day and the moment because it all passes so quickly. Seize the day has critical meaning now for me. Maybe we should all take the time to savor the lives we love—ours and others. Slow down, take the time to call, to text, to visit, to hug, to touch, and to feel, because like a vapor, suddenly it's just not there anymore, and you've lost the chance. It is so final.

May 22nd, 2010

Nine days, most of them in the hospital. Finally, I can stand upright, breathe right and keep stuff in the places it belongs. The compassion and caring of nurses, physicians and ancillary medical staff astounds me. The love and deep caring of my friends and family (and what a huge family I really have), and the support of literally dozens and dozens of those close to me have pulled me through a tough crisis. Thank you for coming here today and for looking in on me. I'm so much better now and you have brought me here.

I continue to recover. Of course, more pills, more liquids keep me mending. Another round of chemicals is coming this week. I pray for the strength to face that ordeal and its aftermath. Soon I will take some time to enjoy a cruise. Five or six days of just laying back and re-absorbing much of the energy that I expended the last two weeks. Just the thought of being able to relax and re-energize is uplifting and helps me as I face another chemo day, the last until after the cruise.

Thank you so much for being here for me, for taking time to give me your love and support. It means all the world to me. Live your life to the fullest! Carpe diem!

May 28th, 2010

Chemo Thursday—Oh, how I've come to fear these days. I appreciate the many people who express their admiration for my "strength". I'm not sure where this strength comes from. Sometimes I think that it's more fear and worry and a false face than it is strength.

I worry sometimes that the pain is just too much and I won't be able to be man enough to bear it. I fear having to rely upon others. Perhaps it's the fear of becoming enslaved to the weaknesses of my body as this awful disease costs me control and subjects me to the humility of things like "Depends". It is those kinds of things that cause doubt to enter my mind. I worry that I might give up and especially that I might give up too soon. I have a deep faith in the Word of God and the lessons and goals that He may have set for me. I fear that giving up too soon will mean that I have lost the opportunity to expend that one last effort, express that one thought or idea, or have denied the physicians the chance to learn from my illness. Giving up too soon may be that I have caused the loss of one thing that may help mankind or this world to become a better place. I fear that my weakness may prevent me from fulfilling the mission that God has set out for me. I think that if the going gets easy that I might be headed downhill, so I persevere. So is perseverance my strength? If so, then it comes from love and faith and wanting to be with my family and my beloved friends as long as God will allow me. Is that strength? If so, fill me with love, with perseverance, and with faith, for then I will be strong. Carpe diem!

June 3rd, 2010

A good friend sent me a beautiful poem written by a poet who recently died of cancer. The name of the poem was "*Time to Say Goodbye*". It set me to thinking (not that I haven't done much thinking over the last year). I sat in my beautiful, flower-filled yard and reflected on this last year and thought about that poem. I'm not going to lie; I came out of this exercise with tears in my eyes and more dedicated to my life than even the day the doctors told me that I have a serious and terminal kind of cancer.

Go somewhere where you can be alone for a short time, or maybe as you lay in your bed tonight. Make sure if there is noise that it is just natural ambient noise. My background noise was the birds and crickets that evening. Ponder this question as I did:

I daydreamed that I had an illness, and God told me that I was going to die tonight as I slept. I begged Him for the chance to tell my loved ones goodbye and to say one last time "I love you" to as many of my friends and family that I could. God said to me, "You have kept Me in your heart and in your mind for all of these years, so I will give you one more day to do what you will before I call you to come to Me".

The question was now before me as I spent my last night and knew that tomorrow was my last gift on earth from God. If I have one day left, and I knew it, what would I do with that day? Dearest beloved friends and family, now ask yourself that question. Ponder it carefully. I may have many days, I may have one. I am compelled to think of tomorrow as the gift of one day that God had promised me. What should I do with it? The poet made some excellent choices, and I thought of some of my own.

I would value things for what they represent, not for what they're worth. I would sleep little and dream of good things while I was awake. I would close my eyes less, for every moment that I had my eyes closed was sixty seconds less of life and light that I would see on this—my last day. I would bare my body and soul to the sunlight and run in it and let it bathe me. I would will the child to do whatever they could do. The poet wishes to give the child wings but not teach them to fly, to allow them to experience learning, and I agree. I have learned and I appreciate that the top of the mountain, although it is the goal, is not as important as how I climbed the mountain. I learned as the poet has expressed, and I believe with all of my heart that I must never look down on another man except when I am extending my hand to help him up. I thank God that I got to see my best friend and his wife receive God's gift of a child. I was given the gift myself to watch my beloved best friends as that child grabbed their fingers, and I knew from that moment on that that little baby boy not only had their fingers but had their hearts, and they were his prisoners forevermore. I know that in my last day that I was not going to hold back my feelings. If I love you, I will tell you that I love you. If you are my friend, I will tell you how much your friendship has meant to me. I will reach out to as many of my friends and my family as I could possibly touch in that last day to tell them thank you for being with me on a part of my wonderful journey through this life. No matter what has happened, for what it's worth, it was worth all the while. I don't think that one day will be enough, but it is the gift that God has given me, and I will do the best I can to deserve every second of that gift of one last day.

Thank you for coming here today. I love you. You are my friend. Carpe diem!

June 11th, 2010

Just a quick entry today, good and faithful friend. I had two chemo injections today. The unfortunate news is that they have discovered some new lesions on my right iliac wing to go along with the destructive mass on my sacroiliac junction. We are formulating the next steps to address the problem. Overall I am feeling very good, much better than I have in a few weeks. I am preparing to leave for my cruise next weekend and then a full-frontal assault on the beast upon my return. I am sleeping reasonably well, and the summer days are keeping my spirits high. Thank God for the support of my staff at work. They make me want to keep up the fight. Thank God for you and for all of my friends and family because I want to stay with you and with your prayers, and with God's will, I shall. We'll talk again when I get back from the cruise. Thank you for being here for me.

June 29th, 2010

I just spent a wonderful week "away from it all"—phones, chemo, medications, physician appointments and day-to-day work all left behind as I traveled off to the Caribbean on my cruise. To the full value of the happiness of a vacation, you have to have someone to share it with. I went with my beautiful wife and nine others of my beloved friends and family. I fully intended to enjoy every single second of this vacation, primarily because of my illness and some of the dismal outlooks given me over the last several months. I truly enjoyed every single second of this vacation, more than I had hoped for. I am convinced that I would not have been so fulfilled had I not been with our little group of travelers.

This trip made me realize that I must take that same approach to living every day of my life. I must intend to enjoy every single moment of living and most of all, I must share the joy of my life and the happiness in my life with others. If I cannot feel the full joy of this life and all the happiness that accompanies it, perhaps it's because I'm not sharing that joy. What, after all, is more contagious than laughter? How can you frown when someone else is smiling? How can you see the dark side when everyone around you sees the light? It's a mindset. It's a devotion to enjoying life and a conscious rejection of the dark and dismal. It is contagious. Listen to the laughter! It's me enjoying the beauty of life and all it has to offer. Listen to my laughter and soon you'll share in the joy of this life too. I vow to share the light, the joy and the happiness so that this wonderful cruise can go on and on.

July 8th, 2010

I won't subject you to my life philosophies today. Today I will step back and give you a picture of where I stand in this battle with the beast—cancer.

I have completed six months of chemotherapy. The oncologist tells me that he wants to give me three more treatments and then a rest of two months. It will be welcome. What really took me out was the month of daily radiation treatments in conjunction with the chemotherapy.

The treatments have helped to manage the beast. At least that's what the doctors say. His reports to me are scary, but he says it's what he expected and where we expected to be at this point. I have survived for a year and two months, so what he's doing must be right. The oncologist shows me bone scans and x-rays that show the picture of the miserable beast before and after the radiation. He sits on my pelvis, his main body is in my prostate. He is an ugly thing. The doctor gives it the name "destructive mass". The chemo and radiation have stunted his growth but have not prevented the beast from putting out tentacles. We see lesions on my right pelvic wing. They look like abnormal bumps on what should be smooth bone. They also look like little caves where the bone has broken down. The bumps and caves are abnormal bone cells and are very weak, leaving me at high risk for pelvic fractures. That is why I have a strict lifting limitation. I can appreciate the concern after staring at the beast and his destruction. To a lesser degree, the beast has little niches in my lumbar vertebrae and my ribs. They appear to be nongrowing but also nonshrinking. At least they are not currently a concern.

The upside to this is that we seem to have this thing under control. It makes me cautiously happy. The downside is the side effects of the treatments. People tell me that I look good. I appreciate that. It takes monthly chemo treatments and an occasional injection of chemicals, a month of daily radiation and twenty-three pills each day to look this way. As much as I may look good, most of the time, I am in a great deal of pain. The beast's location means constant lower back pain, controlled by 24-7 Morphine, backed up by occasional, as needed, instant release Morphine (my rescue med). The pain radiates into my hips and down my legs, making it difficult to walk and often affects my balance. Going up and down the steps is excruciating. Nighttime is the worst. I wake up usually hourly, and most nights have to supplement my overnight Morphine with instant release Morphine along with 240 milligrams of Naproxen. I'm usually exhausted by morning and struggle to get up and get moving. The doctor says he'd rather I didn't work, at least cut back to no more than twenty hours a week. I am forbidden risky behaviors like taking ambulance calls. (That is one of my life's passions—how do you handle such a restriction and stay upbeat?)

I was extremely depressed at the end of radiation. I don't mind telling you. I had constant diarrhea and at times uncontrollable nausea and vomiting. I even spent a week in the hospital in an effort to gain control. I have lost virtually all of my body hair except for the hair on my head. (Isn't that a little contrary to the popular image of a chemo/radiation patient?) Parts of me have atrophied and I feel like I've lost my manhood and masculinity completely. The diarrhea was so uncontrolled that for a few weeks, I was forced to wear a diaper-like garment. How demeaning is that? I guess you can see how one gets so depressed.

Despite all of that, I've had the love and support of you—of my true friends, of my loved ones and of my family. The diapers are gone now. I've been able to travel and continue to work (although I am going against doctor's orders to do so—I refuse to curl up in a corner and wait do die). I am alive and I love life. I am willing to continue to fight this beast in the hopes of gaining more time in a life that I love. I may have to curtail some things I like to do in the future and undergo some more depressing and demeaning things. As long as I have the support of all that think of me, then I owe a strong fight in return. I'm okay and I appreciated your tolerance of my mood swings and depression, as well as your joy when my news is good. Thank you for coming here today. I just wanted you to know, I didn't want to worry or depress you. I have lots of fight left and, God willing, lots of years with you.

July 19th, 2010

If you have faith in the promises of Jesus and love God, pray for me today. If you do not have a belief, then allow me to pray for your devotion to our friendship and your strength to add to mine, which is wavering at the moment. Today's battle is taking its toll on me. If God were to open Heaven's door and say to me, "I will offer you everlasting peace and pain-free sleep today, or I will offer you the chance to continue the battle, knowing that you can still do good for mankind in your life", I would be hard-pressed to turn down the former on this day.

My pain is tremendous, and this is the worst few days of the war thus far. I haven't slept in three days more than ten minutes at a time. The pain in my back, hips, and legs is nearly unbearable and certainly exhausting. I'm not sure I have the strength to tell my God that I will choose to give what I can to help man understand this beast. I have so many pain medications on board, perhaps it's confusing my thoughts. Stay with me, beloved friends. I'm sure this isn't the worst of the battles I will engage the beast in, but it is very hard today. With your love and devotion to our companionship in this part of the journey that we are sharing together in this life, I will survive this day, this battle, and go on to serve the lessons set for me. Not my will but His be done. Thank you.

July 21st, 2010

I am, I live, I love my life. My pain is behind me once again, and I have overcome it. I fear and loathe my weakness in those time of pain crisis. As I came out of this recent exertion, I have learned that it's only for a short time that I have to endure the pain. Eventually it subsides. I've learned how much I can bear. I've learned that I can lean on others. I've learned to trust others, my friends, my loved ones. I now understand because that support, your devotion to me, is a huge part of the strength I need to fight the battle. I am not in this alone. Today I feel stronger than ever and I am so grateful for every message of caring and hope that I received over the last two days. You are my strength and now I realize it.

Something that Faulkner wrote came back to me as I reflected on this experience. He said, *"Given the choice between the experience of pain and nothing, I would choose pain"*. I feel a bit foolish today because I almost lost my faith last weekend, the pain was so great. I almost wished for nothing. What a waste of life that would have been. Faulkner was absolutely right. You can't give up because nothing is just that. By giving up, you have accomplished nothing. You have given nothing back to man. You end up with nothing. How sad and selfish is that?

August 7th, 2010

It really has been a couple of good weeks. The pain has been well under control up until a couple of days ago. I have come to understand that there will be good for a period. It is the script I have to follow. The only limit to my realization of tomorrow's happiness and peace will be my doubts of today. I will move forward with strong faith. Hope is putting faith to work when doubting would be easier. I believe in the sun even if it isn't shining. I believe in love even when I'm alone. I believe in God even when He is silent.

I have taken much time through this whole affair to look around me. I've watched others with much more reason to doubt life that I have and yet they persist. Where does their strength and faith come from? Edwin Chapin once said, "*Out of suffering have emerged the strongest souls. The most massive characters in all of time are seared with scars of life*". I know that I am not seared with scars. My life has given me some bad times, and I too have some scars; but when I look closely at those around me, I have so much more to be thankful for because my life has been good. Now I just want to reach out and say to those who suffer more pain than I, you have helped me by your example. I have determined that now when I offer to help someone, that if I am going to reach out a hand, I will be willing to extend my whole arm. I will only pass through this life one time. If there is any kindness I can show or any good thing that I can do for my fellow being, let me do it now as I'm not going to pass this way again.

The only time I really become discouraged is when I think of all the things that I would like to do and then think of what little time I have in which to do them. Nearly every man who develops an idea or pursues a dream works it to the point where it looks impossible and then gets discouraged. I've learned that that is not the place to become discouraged because, at that point, I am on the verge of success. I will live. I will love. I will have faith even when the sun is not shining.

August 20th, 2010

Wow. It's been a tough few days. I may have overdone work this week and the effort now demands payment in pain. Now though I know that when the pain has backed down that I have good days ahead. Today I feel fine, like I want to dance and sing. The ups and downs are taxing, but the ups are so pleasant and welcome that I don't mind the tough days so much anymore.

I had my consult this week—three fractures in my pelvis. They are healing, albeit slowly. There are new shadows on my right femoral head and acetabulum. We will stop chemo for two months—agreed, no radiation for now in an effort to save bone marrow. They've increased my pain medication doses. I will watch closely over the next two months and report changes immediately to the oncologist who promises to jump in as soon as it is needed. It was a reassuring visit and the plan is sound.

I am looking forward to some time off over the next couple of weeks and a great vacation train trip to the Midwest with my wife in November. I am at peace. I have my family, my friends and all the love piled high upon me. There is no better medication than these things.

August 30th, 2010

I was feeling a bit down today. I had a great weekend—a beautiful wedding and a day at the fair. It was great to see the joy of a new couple with their whole life ahead of them. The bride and groom are special to me and that they would invite me to share in the joy of their special day is a part of my joy in life. At the same time on the same day, Mickie and I shared our sixth wedding anniversary and this couple was thoughtful enough to take time from their day of wonder to acknowledge ours.

The day at the fair was awesome too, although we had to rest several times. That's the part that has me down. As a young man in school, I ran track and played baseball. I was on the city softball league and bowled twice a week. Now I bring a cane for long walks and have to rest so many times. I loved the fair, but I paid last night and this morning. I took the meds for the pain and survived, but I lament for times past and the health of youth.

A song came on the radio today. It struck home and surely it helped me on a down day. It goes like this:

> *I'm only human, I'm just a man. Help me*
> *believe in what I could be and all that I am. Show*
> *me the stairway I have to climb. Lord, for my sake,*
> *teach me to take one day at a time.*

One day at a time, sweet Jesus, that's all I'm asking from You. Just give me the strength to do every day what I have to do. Yesterday's gone, sweet Jesus, and tomorrow may never be mine. Lord, help me today, show me the way, one day at a time.

How true are the words. Yesterday is gone and I mustn't dwell upon it. Tomorrow may never be mine, so I must concentrate on living this day. It is faith in the word and promises of God through Jesus that gives me the strength. I felt so much better after I thought things through, and so on I go one day at a time.

September 5th, 2010

I apologize for the melancholy in my last writing here. I look at the inspiring messages that you write to me, words of encouragement and support, feelings of love and empathy, and then despite all you do for me, I sink into melancholy. Your words (thank you, Jahn, I love you!) help to open my eyes wide. When I wrote of living one day at a time, I selfishly was thinking of my own pain and my own battle with this ugly consuming beast. What I failed to grasp, although I know it, was that we all, each one of us, are guaranteed only this moment in time. None of us knows for sure that there is a tomorrow for ourselves. Sometimes I need to stop and think more of others. We are all on this trip through life together, each in our own seat but all on the same vehicle. Each of us has our own stop to get off, and none of us can ride forever.

My difficulty with this beast has taught me more lessons than just about any other experience in my life. I wish that I could answer each and every one who has given their message of caring for me in my struggle—as of today, 4,999! And yet each of the nearly five thousand has good and bad, bright and dark days, love and heartbreak, peace and turmoil in their life. I'm not alone. Despite the despicable changes the beast has wrought on my physical being, the changes it has brought to me in terms of human insight are positives that in the end will help me as I try to spread the message that love will survive the beast. Peace will survive the beast. And, God has promised, I will survive the beast even after it has consumed this body.

I promise myself and you that I will not allow my mind to become entrapped in melancholy. I will find ways to encourage and support everyone around because I got the message last week. I am not alone in this, and I recognize that we each have only one day at a time. Thank you all, 4,999 times, for your visit and encouragement and love.

September 13th, 2010

Dearest reader, my friend, who is with me today, thank you. I'm afraid that I don't have any words of enlightenment, but please hear my cry in this private place and understand.

I have grappled with the beast for three days now and I am afraid that I have entered a dark depression. I will heed help, for death is in my head. It dominates my thoughts and I can't think of much else. The constant thoughts of death are making it hard for me to think and function well at work, at home, in everything I do. I cling to the promises of my God and beseech Him to be with me and not to abandon me now. Death has filled my waking and doesn't allow me to sleep. I think I'm going to need help. Thankfully I'll see the doctors on Wednesday and maybe they can help to chase death from my head. A CT scan was done today to find where the beast has gone—not far—because the pain he is creating tells me that he is gnawing at my bones and my soul. Oh, God, dear God, please don't be far from me, please hear my cry today—but it is Your will and not mine and I will bow to that always.

I am so sorry, my kind and caring visitor, to subject you to this when all you have done is to come to support me and encourage me. I have slid into the depths and fear the climb back up that I cannot make it. Your visit means all the world to me.

October 1st, 2010

The news is not good today. Cancer has appeared high in my spine, in my chest and shoulders, and the beast is ravaging my pelvis. I have to see the oncologist "as soon as possible," the PA said on the phone today. We can't wait. "New chemo, more radiation is in order," she said. The doctors want me to quit, no more work, no more driving, no more strenuous exercise to preserve my bones, my strength, my life.

I will not quit.

It hurts me more when well-meaning people leave me out of things that I've always done. Teaching others, helping where I can at my place of employment, working around the yard, helping my friends and family with "projects", having fun with my nephews and nieces. If people, whom I love and I hope love me, leave me out of these things for "my own good," then there is no point to continue this struggle. But I'm here to tell you, I will not quit.

I have to work. The work I do is to help others. Maybe it's not safe to climb on ambulances or to try to calculate med doses in a critical situation, so I won't do anything to hurt anyone. But what I can do is to help others that work with me and for me to understand the things a medic needs to know in order to help others.

I will not quit.

I have to be involved if my best friend is working on our apartments or helping his folks. Please don't leave me out "for my own good".

I will not quit.

I refuse to curl up in a ball on a bed or couch and preserve my body. I will use my body and I will use my knowledge and I will continue to do what I can to make life easier and better for my fellow man.

I will not quit.

I refuse to give it up.

I will not quit no matter what the docs want me to do.

God, please be with me. I will not quit.

October 17th, 2010

I visited my oncologist and urologist yesterday after a battery of tests over the last week. Having been told by the doctors that the beast (cancer) has spread his tentacles into the bones of my chest and shoulders, I feared the worst. The doctors were wonderful, fantastic. The battery of tests revealed that the beast has not invaded my bladder or colon, my lungs or liver or other soft tissue. It is the best news that I have heard. The oncologist is confident that the new chemo we are using this week and next will control the "plaques" that have appeared in my sternum, ribs and scapula. He was so upbeat (Did you say oncologist and upbeat in the same breath?) that I came home riding high on a cloud.

I rested after the treatments as I must because they are physically taxing. While I sat here staring at the black and quiet television screen, I started thinking about my life. I believe in angels and I believe in humanity. I look for good in everything I see. Some many years ago, I promised myself that I would work the rest of my life to the betterment of humans and earth. As I reviewed that little promise, I remembered when I made it; I started thinking about my own life.

We all have those things in life, mostly forgotten in the fog of time that we know were morally wrong—worse, something that we have done that resulted in harm or hurt to another human. In my deepest heart and most secret mind, I kept thinking of two things that I fear will keep me from the promise of Jesus that I will share a room in Heaven. Until this moment, I've never ever shared those wrongs with anyone at all. When I think of them, I am so shamed that it drives me to tears (yes, real men do cry as one of my staff inadvertently discovered by accident last week). Each time I speak to God, I ask for His forgiveness for these two transgressions, and yet I find it impossible to forgive myself.

When I was six or seven years old, I lived in Rochester. I was walking at the back part of a playground, outside the fence. I was with a couple of friends. We encountered three small boys, probably five years old or so. For no reason at all, we confronted them and pushed them against the fence. I held the head of one poor child tightly against the chain link. I don't recall what we said to these kids, but I remember (and have remembered daily since then) the absolute terror in the face of this crying child. He begged to be let go, and we did without further harming them. I watched them running off, crying for their mom. We ran off, afraid that now we would have to pay for this horrible act.

My family moved shortly thereafter to the country where I spent the rest of my formative years. I recall that terrible event on the playground vividly and often. The fear, no absolute terror, that I caused that human being brings a knot to my gut and a pain to my heart. I was responsible for that. And for that, I cannot forgive or forget. I thank God, as often as I think of that incident, for taking me out of the urban environment for who knows how I might have turned out. With all of my heart and soul, I wish I could go back and undo that deed. If not undo, then ask for that child to forgive me. Perhaps God, in His mercy, will lay that transgression aside. I don't know. It is hard to think of it. I have not forgiven myself for the evil I had done.

I didn't learn from that experience about my inhumanity to man. About six years ago around Christmas time, I was taking my mother home from a late doctor's appointment. It was getting dark, as it does in New York, around five in the evening. I had had a difficult day at work and wasn't in a particularly good mood. Mother asked if we could take a ride around town to look at the pretty Christmas lights and decorations. Even though it would have taken me twenty minutes, I said no. I took her home even as I took notice of her great disappointment. It was her last Christmas on earth. I will never forgive myself for that second transgression. It was the worst because it was against my mother. God said, "Honor your father and your mother." I cannot forgive myself for she has gone, and it is too late.

So, in the end, think about everything you do. It must be fair, balanced, and good for your fellow human. Go beyond your own feelings, your own illness and your own moment. You may not get another chance because the beast is here and will limit your time to redeem yourself just as he has me.

November 2nd, 2010

It's been a bit of a wild ride over the last month. Scary reports followed by reassurances, followed by new physical "things that don't belong there", followed by even more reassurances. All the time, there's the ever-present pain.

I have learned so much during this battle. I've learned to know myself, to pay attention to how I feel even to the remotest parts of my physical being. That takes careful patience as well as lots of time. I can lay down in my quiet room and explore my mind. I can think about the bottom of my foot and when I do, I can feel it. I can think about my lungs, and breathing becomes pleasurable. I can take a deep breath and feel it all the way down into the lowest lobes of my lungs. I feel the food going through the alimentary canal. I can focus on every area, every cell of this physical body. One would wonder about my sanity. What kind of kook lies in bed and thinks about such crazy things? I do. I do because I went on a search in my body for this beast. I need to know it. I need to know where it is and what it is doing. Only if I know my own cells and tissues when they are normal and "feeling right" will I know where the beast is and what destruction it has wrought. I'm not sure that thinking strong, powerful thoughts against this beast and struggling to think my cells and immune system to undo the beast and its damage are helping; but I have come to know myself, and I feel better about the battle. I have become intimate with my enemy in order to know it.

With all that said, the beast continues to ravage. It has me down oft times. There is a secret to getting back up and fighting back, especially in the lowest of low times. The secret, as I have discovered in the battle, is friends. I'm not talking about that casual one that gives you a pat on the shoulder or a handshake and says, "Call me anytime". I'm not talking about the friend who moves as I move and nods when I nod; my shadow does that very well. I'm talking about the friend that just shows up on my porch at 10:30 at night when she knows I've had a bad day with the beast. She doesn't call ahead, but she drives over and sees me sitting alone on my front porch. She takes the time and stops just to sit by my side and to give me a heartfelt, deep human hug. That friend could be—is—my niece. I'm talking about a friend who doesn't tell me that I can call anytime if I need help around the yard or house, he just shows up one morning and calmly goes about mowing my lawn. I'm talking about the friend—a cousin—who "reads between the lines" in my Facebook posts and then calls immediately because she recognizes anguish. She spends the next hour helping me out of the pit. There are so many others that I could name. The friends just keep showing up. They walk into my office and sit down and just make small talk. And when they get done, they put their arm around my shoulder and just give a squeeze without saying another word. That kind of friendship needs no words. Silence is sometimes the real conversation between friends. It's not the saying but the never needing to say that counts. True friendship—it has no survival value, rather it is one of those things that give value to survival. When it hurts to look back, and you're afraid to look ahead, you can look beside you, and your true friend will always be there. Most people come and go in your life, but only friends leave a print in your heart. I value a friend who looks at his calendar when I need someone close. I cherish the friend who, for me, does not even consult his calendar.

Thank God for my friends. Thank God for you. By being comfortable with myself and having my true friends and family so close by, I do not fear the beast. Because of you, I will continue to take on the beast—not my will but His. Thank you for being here today for me, my friend.

November 5th, 2010

Yesterday, November 4th, I became confused, weak and unbalanced and had vision disturbances shortly after I woke up. It seemed to ease a bit and I went to work. I had an oncologist appointment, and while being examined, these signs appeared again, more intense. The alarmed oncologist insisted I go immediately to the emergency room just on the other side of the building. There, after some testing and a CT scan, I was diagnosed with a transient ischemic attack (TIA), a kind of stroke. I was admitted to the hospital and underwent a battery of tests.

The CT scan demonstrated that it was indeed a TIA (a small stroke) versus an obstructive or hemorrhagic stroke (CVA). While searching for the cause of my stroke, they discovered a "lesion" on the temporal lobe of my brain. I was devastated. The beast has made itself known to me, up close and personal.

I had a follow-up MRI today, along with a thoracic echo and a carotid ultrasound. The good news is that a full-blown stroke is ruled out and my carotid arteries and heart seem okay. Furthermore, they are not sure of the nature of the lesion. The radiologist and neurologist will read the MRI tonight. If it is the beast, we will radiate it. If it is not the beast, we will breathe a sigh of relief. Tonight I turn to God and place myself in His hands. Perhaps the TIA was His guidepost to lead us to the beast early enough to destroy it in my brain. Perhaps it is a false alarm and a harmless anomaly. I will know shortly.

The entry I wrote a few days ago about friends was a message to help anyone who came here recently to be with me. It was meant to help them recognize the need to care and nurture your friendships, your loved ones, and all that you care for in life before it is too late. It was intended to being those who read of my struggle the message that if you consider yourself a friend to anyone, then you must be a true friend and give your all to your friendship. It wasn't intended to be about me and my struggle; it was intended to say that we must take care of each other and treasure each other every minute of every day. It was intended to say we must not pay lip service to being there for each other, but instead we must be true to our words, to live up to our words. We must be, whether we are asked or not—for if we truly care about someone else, we will always recognize their needs, no matter how busy our own life is, we must set aside our calendar when someone we love is in need and just go to them. Since there is no greater treasure on this earth than having friends, never lose a chance to make and take care of them. We must recognize that before it is too late, for the beast is here now. The message I wished to have conveyed last week was that I am so blessed with so many true friends. They all came forward again this last couple of days, and once again, I know the deep love of friendship and family. May our hearts never come apart. Thank God. Thank you.

November 12th, 2010

Choice is completely in our own hands. The choices I make will have consequences for good or for bad, not only in my life but for everyone who may touch my life. That makes choices a concept that I am compelled to make with the greatest of thought and care.

When I awaken each morning, I make a conscious choice; do I want to be happy, in control, uplifting, or will I let circumstances, pain and disease control the direction of my life and my decisions? I choose the former, knowing that my choice will have a consequence. With determination, I choose to be happy and in control and that that decision will direct my day, my dealings with others and how they respond to me. I choose to have a positive approach. I choose to ignore the pain and limitations from the beast who will ultimately kill me. It is my choice; it is my life; I choose to live.

I will be dead all too soon. That knowledge has been the most important tool I have in making choices about just about everything. People's expectations of me, my pride, my fear of failing, fear of embarrassment all fade away in the face of death, leaving only what is truly important. Remembering that I must soon die helps me focus on those truly important things. There is nothing left that forces me not to follow my heart.

This morning is the first day of the rest of my life, as the saying goes. I have been given today, and with this gift, a choice of how to use it. I can waste it, just let it pass away; or I can use it to help someone. With it, I can choose to enrich another human's knowledge and their life. The choice I make is important because I am exchanging a day of what remains of my life for sake of improving the lot of man, even though it might be just one man. When and if my tomorrow comes, for me today will be gone forever; in its place is something I have left behind. My choice right now is that what I leave behind is something good. I will thus have left this earth and mankind better than I found it.

I will not die an unlived life. I choose to actively participate in life. I choose by that participation to make me less fearful, especially of death. Dawna Markova wrote, "*I will live so that which comes to me as a seed I deliver to another as a blossom and that which is given me as a blossom goes on as fruit*".

This is my choice. I will try to live my last days making choices to deliver the seed as a blossom, and the blossom as a fruit. May this be my legacy—not my will but Yours.

December 18th, 2010

I am feeling pretty good. In the last few weeks, I have been relieved from chemicals and radiation to allow this poor body a chance to relax and catch up. It has been a relief. The doctors are calling me stable for now. I suppose that means we're not falling behind this awful beast even though we don't seem to be progressing in driving it back. In January, I will return to the chemo again, but for now, thank God for the rest.

As I slip through time, sometimes struggling and sometimes just sliding easily along, I've come to realize that as long as I have a "why", I need to live, to continue the struggle. Then the "how" to survive can mean bearing almost anything I need to suffer in order to continue. I have so many "whys". I still see a lot of sense in my life. I have goals to aim for, purpose to my existence and thus a point to living. Life ultimately means taking responsibility for finding the right answer to life's problems and to fulfill the tasks which life constantly sets for me as an individual. Even suffering can be a task set out for me in my unique life, my single and unique task, for we must each suffer in our own way and react in our own way. No one can relieve me of this task nor suffer in my place. The opportunity for me is the way in which I will bear this burden, this task set before me.

I now know that it is necessary for me to face up to the full amount of suffering, the full measure of this unrelenting pain, working to achieve my goals despite the guarantee of my ultimate end. I must try to keep moments of weakness and the useless tears to a minimum. I am not ashamed of tears because I now know that tears bear witness to the courage it takes to suffer, but I must not let the tears be my outlet, for they will distract me from my life's aims and the goals I yet have to reach.

My family, my friends, my coworkers, my students and a certain measure of humanity look to me, for I have proclaimed that I dedicate my life to the betterment of mankind. I still have ways to go and I'm not ready to give up those goals no matter the suffering laid out before me. I am coming up on the second anniversary of the proclamation of the beast's presence in this body. The physicians told me then I had between one and three years of struggle. I choose to continue the struggle for many years to come for the aims and goals that are there for me cannot be achieved in two or three years. I know I can bear the pain and that I will, no matter what it takes, because the "why" is that I don't have time for death, there is much yet to be done.

January 5th, 2011

The last two weeks were wonderful. Time with family and friends during a festive season is as healing as any medicine. Today I woke to brilliant sunshine but not such a good day.

I feel heaviness in my chest and pain in my shoulder. I recognized this old enemy. I felt like I needed fresh air, but I was so weak that I had to lay back and concentrate on breathing. I took a total of three Nitroglycerin tablets before the heaviness resolved. It was another hour before I felt strong enough to get out of bed. In the meantime, the beast was gnawing at my pelvis. I was covered in sweat. I checked my blood glucose—52 mg/dl. That explained the sweating and weakness. A quick peanut butter toast and a glass of milk brought things back to normal. The beast was relentless as I worked to get myself straightened out. About three hours into the battle, I was once again in front of my enemies.

Some mornings are just tougher than others. This was one. Perhaps it was a payback for the excellent holiday season. If so, it was worth it because I was so happy with my loved ones and my so-true friends. There is my reward and my treasure in this life.

I still feel out of sorts. I came to work and expect things to improve over the next several hours. If not, back to my doctors for some insight and advice. The beast is working hard on my back today. I fight back with strong medications and very strong resolve. Carpe diem!

January 19th, 2011

I listened to a recording of a woman saying a prayer this week. It struck a chord with me close to home. Within her plea to God, she said, "Forgive me if I don't quite get things right, dear Lord. I've never been this old before".

Boy, isn't there a lot of truth in just that little phrase. I was having a one-on-one visit with Dylan last weekend. I had so much fun. As I contemplated the prayer from that lady, it set me to thinking about why I was having so much fun with a six-year-old. We started the snowblower because there was a big drift in front of the garage door. We absolutely had to clear that drift because we needed to get the tractor out so we could hang up the caution tape over the entrances to the house. What made this so much fun was the incredible delight Dylan had in every single thing we were doing. Why did Dylan keep saying, "Uncle Ken, what does this lever do?" or "What will happen when I push this peddle, Uncle Ken?" It dawned on me today that my fun was coming from his delight in seeing something new for the very first time. More importantly, he saw a huge number of new things that I took for granted because I saw them before or used the tool before or knew what the tool would do. To Dylan, every single moment we spent together, before we went in to get a cup of hot chocolate, was a brand-new experience, a new adventure.

What a lesson I learned from that six-year-old that day. All it took—all it takes—is to pay attention to what is right in front of me even if I've done it before. The new sensations, the fresh air that I've never breathed before (because that 500 cc of air had never been in my lungs before that moment that I took it in). Wow! I've never been 59 years and 178 days old before. I'm only that old today, never before and never again. That peanut butter sandwich I had today, even though it's Jif, contains peanuts that have never been on my taste buds before. Each and every thing I hear, each thing I touch or do or smell or taste or experience, is in some way the first time because it's in a different time, room, airstream, light. Even though I've done it before, it is now a new experience for me. It is if I pay attention to it. It is if I enjoy it and delight in the fact that it's brand-new.

I have chemo today. As I battle this ugly, unrelenting beast, I am doing so with a fresh approach, a renewed faith and a renewed vow. For the first time, I know the beast just a bit better. I will look at my life just the way Dylan did that day and just the way that wonderful woman did in her prayer. No matter what this day, this disease, this life brings for me to experience today, it is the first time I have experienced it just this way. I will enjoy and learn from it. It is my way to live my life fully. Carpe diem!

February 16th, 2011

"Ignis aurum probat, miseria fortes viros." The Latin phrase says that fire tests gold, misfortune tests the strength of man. These past few weeks have tested me more than I ever thought I could bear.

I continue to have pain. I guess that's the beast's gift to me as he gnaws away at this poor vessel that I inhabit. A week ago, I began having pain in my lower legs (some place new). Suddenly I had a couple of days where I was having trouble breathing on exertion. It progressed to vertigo, a feeling that I was going to pass out. Any movement at all caused a racing heart and increased difficulty breathing. One of my forever friends, who happens to be a registered nurse, came to my home at the request of my poor, worried wife. Lisa, RN, took a look at me as I struggled on the stairs and made it clear that decisions were being made. Before I knew it, my own ambulance corps brought an ambulance to my door along with a supervisor car. I got to experience firsthand the expertise, the empathy and the caring of these paramedics. Despite the fact that I was their boss, something that might cause some to become timid, I was rapidly assessed, treated, and transported to the hospital.

I was admitted to the ICU for four days. Tests showed that I had clots in both of my legs and that one of the clots had moved into my lungs, a pulmonary embolism. That pretty much explained all of my signs and symptoms. I am now on Plavix, Coumadin, and Lovenox, meant to dissolve the clots and keep my blood "thin". Another week of "bed rest" and I returned to work.

No sooner did I get back that the beast reared his ugly head again. This week, it has vastly increased pain in my lower back, which has spread to my hips and down the back of both legs. The pain is so bad that I can hardly stand. Walking is difficult and stairs are excruciating. Off I went to the oncologists today, looking for answers and help with pain. X-rays, bone scans, numerous blood tests are upcoming for the rest of this week. The dose of Morphine is increased until I feel like I'm in a fog. The orders are for bed rest until the bone scan and a new plan is laid out for me by the doctors.

I have returned to work. I refuse to curl up in a corner and wait to die. I can suffer pain sitting in my chair, contributing to the successful company that my team and I have built. I can suffer that pain as well at work as I can at home. At work, I feel like I am helping, contributing. The support given me by my staff is beyond belief. My wife and my best (forever) friends await me every night and every morning to ensure that I am getting what I need and getting where I need to be. My brothers and their wives and my nieces and nephews are godsends.

If misfortune tests the strength of man, then I have been sorely tested this past month. Without the support of my staff, my friends and my family, I would have taken that advice to curl up in bed rest long ago; but this struggle would have ended long ago too. God bless all who are in this together with me in the hands of God. *"Ignis aurum probat, miseria fortes viros."* (Fire tests gold; adversity tests strong men.)

February 23rd, 2011

A whole week of tests, needles, bone scans, x-rays, CT and MRI, still in pain—sometimes it's tolerable and other times excruciating. I am weary. I'm not afraid to admit that sometimes I weep. I really believe that in order to see life more clearly, we occasionally need our eyes to be washed by tears.

As each day passes, more challenges are placed before me, old pain, new pain in new places—trouble breathing, sometimes not even able to lift myself from the bed or a chair. It's hard to keep up the strength to do this battle. I think about what's ahead. Ultimately it is death. But ultimately, death is for each one of us. I will continue to live, to fight to enjoy the gifts that have been given me. So many people tiptoe through life so carefully to arrive safely at death. Death is more universal than life; everyone dies, but not everyone lives. It is our individual choice. Death is not the opposite of life; it exists as a part of life. I'm not afraid of dying, I just don't want to.

Still the time must come when the final door opens. I'll find my way through this life, this struggle, through night and day because when that final door does open, beyond that door is peace. Of that I am sure and just as sure I believe there'll be no more tears in heaven.

I'm so glad that you're with me. I am so relieved to have you by my side. I know I must be strong and carry on. I know that because you are by my side, and you help me stand. When that door does open and I am gone, know that death leaves a heartache no one can heal, but love leaves a memory no one can steal. Death ends a life, not a relationship. Carpe diem!

March 24th, 2011

I had a conversation today with a fireman. His fire company had just lost a member after a long battle in trying to recover from catastrophic burns. The fight lasted for the better part of two years. I questioned the fireman in front of me, "Who are you crying for, yourself or your deceased friend?" I felt comfortable talking about death and dying with this grieving man because not only have I experienced it myself as a paramedic and medical teacher, but I have been on the same path now for two years myself. I'm not an expert, but I have learned many, many things about myself and humanity and death and dying over the last two years.

Harriet Beecher Stowe once wrote, "*The bitterest tears shed over graves are for words left unsaid and deeds left undone.*" I read those words many years ago and never did they have greater meaning until my dad died twenty plus years ago. I cried and grieved then. I was angry with myself. I realized that I wasn't crying for the suffering that my father might have experienced in his final moments on earth, but instead I was angry and crying because I never got the chance to say I love you. It wasn't manly; it just wasn't done, men telling men I love you. What a foolish person I was. He was my father, he was my friend, he was a role model for me. I blew it. Now I could only rely on my faith that there was a life beyond this earthly existence and that my dad could hear my pleas asking for forgiveness because, "Dad, I do love you and I miss you terribly." Like my fireman friend, I lamented a lost opportunity to tell another human being that I do care, that I do love, even another man. Because that love is not a sexual thing, it's a human thing. I vowed to never waste another opportunity to express my gratitude for another human being's love, caring, counsel, or closeness no matter what, who, or their gender.

I am lucky in my battle against a beast that I know will win the fight in the end. My fireman's now deceased friend was lucky as well. We are (and were) lucky because we both knew well ahead of time the fact of our inevitable demise even though we don't know the exact time it approaches. I get to see as many friends and family and humans as I can to share my life's experiences, joys, failures, and successes. I get to hug them, kiss them and tell them goodbye and they get to tell me how much they care and love me and they get to tell me goodbye. Most of us don't get that opportunity.

The battle is easier to fight, and the inevitable end is easier to understand. Closure is closer at hand when finally he left, and it will be when I finally depart. I thank God for the opportunity He has given me to say goodbye, to express my love for my fellow man and to my family and loved ones. God gave this gift of time to that fireman and the fireman gave his family and colleagues the same gift. Now we all can be in peace, knowing that our existence is known and appreciated and that my love has been expressed now while there is time. I am blessed. The fireman was blessed. I hope that those whose lives we have touched understand the peace that this long battle has at last given us.

Ancient Egyptians believed that upon death, they would be asked two questions and their answers would determine whether they could continue their journey into the afterlife. The first was, "Did you find joy?" The second was, "Did you bring joy?" I hope to answer both in the affirmative in regard to my blessed life. When the time comes that I pass through that door and you surely will have tears, I ask you, "Why should I be out of your mind because I'm out of your sight? Remember, I will still be here as long as you hold me in your memory." Remember me.

April 30th, 2011

I have met the beast face-to-face, and then head-on. We have done battle. For now, it is over. I am left weak and in pain. I not only survived but have damaged the beast (dare I say overcome). God indeed has guided me to this physician but then guided that talented hand to ensure that I would still walk and function as a man. A mere millimeter to the right or left would have me paralyzed, unable to move, or walk or even control my bowels. Look and see the space of a millimeter. It is only the width of the space between two letters in this work. The shaking of a hand, an itch on the nose, a blink of the eye, or momentary distraction would give the beast the final say. The beast did not have the final say. The surgeon did not come off the true mark that he was to follow. In the end, despite beast and man, God has spoken!

I endured about four hours of surgery and a few extra in recovery on Monday, the 25th of April, almost exactly two years to the day that we first detected the beast. The surgeon is a renowned expert on brain and spinal cord tumors. He skillfully removed almost all of the tumor that had destroyed spinal lumbar vertebrae 3 and 4 and continued on to take all the residual bone fragments, relieving the pressure on my spinal cord, which has given me agonizing and incessant pain in my hips and legs. There was some repair to lumbar 2 and 5 (S-1). He is confident of the fact that we have given me the relief that I so badly wanted, needed and prayed for. He reassures me that the war is not over, but we have won a major battle.

I stood and walked on Tuesday morning. There was no leg and hip pain! I was weak and still am weak. Because of my related health issues, I stayed in hospital until Thursday afternoon. I walked out of that building into bright sunshine and a warm spring breeze. I had a little setback on Friday, spending most of the day quite out of it as a result of the numerous medications I am taking.

I got up this morning and showered and shaved. I walked my dog, even if it was only a couple hundred yards. Today I sit at home and recover my strength. I think of all the people that sent mighty prayers upward, over eighty-eight greeted me on Facebook on Monday alone and a larger number over the next few days. I will meet with my surgeon on Tuesday next. Over the next week or so, I will see the other skilled doctors who worked together as we fought this awful beast. I asked each and every physician only one question at the beginning of this battle and I told each that I wanted only a simple yes or no answer. The question was, "Do you believe in God?" To a man, they each replied with an empathic "yes." There was no need for me to ask any other questions.

I leave you now, dear loved one, dear reader. I thank you for being here for me today and for being among those whose pleas to God were answered. I will be back after I visit with the physicians this coming week. Carpe diem!

June 28th, 2011

So here I am eight weeks later. It has been a nightmare for six of those weeks. I spent almost the entire month of May in hospital. At one point, I lost track of every moment for a week. Sunday, Monday, Tuesday, Wednesday and Thursday are gone from my life. My wife says, "You were out of your mind". What truth there is in that statement. I was not in my body. The beast almost won that week. At one point, they hung blood and used fluids and medications to maintain my blood pressure. I was in acute renal failure and spiraling downward. I knew nothing. My family was called to my bedside and stayed with me for many hours. I had care twenty-four hours. We beat the beast down. I survived and have returned.

We have turned another corner and I'm feeling better than I have in a few months. Still, the beast has caused complications. I will undergo a probe, a scope into my GU track and bladder. Renal and liver tests are underway. The scope is Friday and within ten days, a TURP (transurethral resection of the prostate) procedure to help me empty my bladder. It means a urinary catheter for at least a week and the possibility of incontinence for weeks to come. But I am alive, and the beast has not won yet. My PSA is up a bit. I had chemo injections last week and look forward to a couple of months before any more chemo treatments. It may be a pleasant summer. Things are looking up. I hope it holds. May and June are a blur and a nightmare. My family and friends, my fellow workers and staff, and the faculty at EMS and FLCC deserve a rest from worry and from cooking my dinner, mowing my lawn, taking care of my house, yard and me. Thank God for each and every one who prayed, cooked, worked and worried. Thank you, each and everyone. I am looking forward to a relaxing summer and I offer that to you as well while I recover from this terrible beast's assault.

July 13th, 2011

Today—bloodwork, ultrasounds, bone scan and CT, looking closely at my vasculature for DVTs. There is a proposal to do surgery to relieve obstruction in my urethra, but it can't be done if I have clots in my legs. The tests today will tell us if there is a need to resolve the DVTs (deep vein thrombosis) or if we can go forward with the surgery. I have a feeling of pressure in my groin. We are checking to see if there is growth in my pelvis and right hip causing that. It is painful, making it very difficult to walk. Thank God that the excruciating pains in my legs were resolved with the previous surgery. I don't know if I could bear having this groin pain along with that pain. I hope and pray that there is not a bone tumor that invades my ischium and acetabulum. The tests will help us to know. So, as I sit here awaiting the next scan and the dye to take effect, I worry. I don't know why. *Is est quisi is est* (It is what it is) and we'll react to whatever is found. I believe in angels and the work they do for God. I believe that I have angels with their hands on me to reassure me for God's plan. Today is only twenty-four hours and soon it will be over. Then I will know the next path I must follow.

August 21st, 2011

Tomorrow, August 22, 2011, at 7:30 a.m., I will once again place my life and body into the hands of the surgeon. This time is different. This time, I am fearful. I'm not afraid of the surgeon or the surgery. I am not afraid to continue to battle this awful beast inside. There is something nearby. There is a presence, a shadow that has been with me for more than a year. It is a darkness that I can see day and night. It is not threatening, it has no face, and it has no voice. But the shadow, the presence, is not reassuring; it is unsettling. I have come to fear it.

I was in Clifton Springs Hospital two weeks ago and was quite ill. I woke up suddenly in the middle of the night and sat up on the side of my bed. The shadow was with me as it normally is. The shadow was darker than usual. I had a very uneasy feeling. I was getting up to use the bathroom. The shadow moved closer to me, and for the first time in the year, it has been with me, actually touched me. I suddenly became nauseous. I hurried into the bathroom and vomited. I felt weak and I don't mind telling you, dearest friend, I was scared. I returned to my bed and sat down. The shadow moved closer again. I felt that it wanted to get on the bed beside me. I quickly got up and sat in the chair against the wall and there I spent the rest of the night. The nurses asked if I was okay and if I wanted to return to my bed. I could not and would not. The shadow went back to its normal distance and has not accosted me again since. It is still with me though.

The vision was so real. The nausea and vomiting were not a dream. Now I fear that the shadow will follow me into the operating room tomorrow. I believe in angels and their work in the name of God for the benefit of man. I pray with all my heart that God will send an angel to stand between my operating table and the shadow tomorrow morning. I pray that the angel will stop the shadow from interfering with the surgeon. I pray to my God that He will not allow the shadow to get on the table with me.

I have never felt so apprehensive in all my life. I am not a man to cower from anything, but this shadow is so real and this vision seems to live. It may not be so for me, for this shadow's name is death.

Pray for me, my friend, that God may guide the hand of the doctor and that I may awaken with an angel by my side and the shadow once again fading into the background.

August 23rd, 2011

It is Tuesday, August 23rd. I have won this battle this day. The shadow which has followed me for a year is still there, but it is diminished. I am awake again and my fear is gone. Thank you, dearest friend, for your prayers and support through this most difficult time.

September 12th, 2011

I've had a tough month after my most recent surgery. Following closely is a shadow, the same shadow that was with me in my room in

Clifton Springs Hospital. It was in my bedroom last week, standing next to my bed. A picture of my wife and I, which is on the shelf at the head of the bed, fell over and woke me up. I was having some difficulty drawing a deep breath and saw the shadow standing there. I was able to get up and turn on the lights—*all of them*. I don't know what the shadow wants but it leaves me with a depressing, cold feeling. Was it just a nightmare? I don't know, but it shook me to the very depths of my soul.

I am having trouble with control of my body functions. The cancer in my spine has rendered muscles and nerves in my pelvis and associated organs "nonfunctional" as the urologist put it. I must wear adult underwear. I don't even know when it is time to change them until I become saturated. Is this the way I must live now? It is sad that one spends a lifetime getting education, maturing, gaining life experience, making friendships, and building professional relationships only to return to the role of a helpless infant.

There are days when I believe that it would be easier for me to simply fade away, leaving my family, friends and loved ones with a memory of a strong and dedicated man rather than a man who walks with pain and difficulty, cannot tend to his own lawn and yard and cannot even control his own body.

I put in my notice to end my career a couple of weeks ago after I became "wet" during an important meeting with medical and community leaders. I cannot keep doing this, I think. My boss looked me square in the eye and said, "No, you aren't going to quit". I wasn't quite prepared for that response. I agreed to stay on but to cut back on the hours I work. It has helped but not completely.

My God, is this the way I must live out my life? I will battle the beast. I will live with the pain. I know that the beast is consuming my body and its controls, but to steal my pride and my confidence is just unexpected. I pray it gets better, but each day is a true struggle with my feelings. Even as the beast eats away my physical body now, it has begun an assault on my mind. The medications to control this pain do just that but leave me in a fog, often confused and unsure of myself. This is the greatest struggle: to lose my sanity, my mind. I fear it more than anything else. Thank you, my friend, for staying near me, for hearing me and understanding me. Not my will but Yours be done.

September 22nd, 2011

Why am I so tormented? What is the purpose that I am suffering the humility, embarrassment, and pain of this illness? Those are the questions that I've asked myself over the last two weeks. As I laid in my bed last night, these thoughts were running through my head. My medications are playing havoc with my thinking. The beast is wrecking this body. The shadow waits in the corner. I lay here wondering, thinking, worrying.

Then it came to me. What purpose is there in all of this? There has to be a way that I can use this to help others understand illness and suffering beyond their control. It is a lesson to me, and now I can share. By sharing my experiences and the love and support that I've received from family and friends, I can help others to stand before this beast and say, "Is that all you've got?" To the shadow, "I'm not afraid of you." To the doctors' medications, "Let's take a closer look and see if I need all of this or at least in the quantities you have prescribed." For me, "How can I take better care of this failing body so that I feel better, look better and take advantage of all of those things that are enjoyable still left to me, even if I can't do all the things that I used to?" If I can't play baseball anymore, won't the game be almost as enjoyable if I can be the umpire? Of course it can. There is brightness to every day. There are tons of things that I can still do. There are lots of lessons I can share with both the ill and the healthy to make their lives better and more enjoyable.

So in the end, I'm not so tormented, not so depressed, but instead I'm renewed. I have a purpose and I accept that new challenge and promise to live out this life with a new attitude. I can help. I can teach. I can be of use because how I portray myself can give others hope in the knowledge that we're not so unhealthy until at last God says, "Enough my beloved. You have done well, and mankind is better because of it". Carpe diem!

November 15th, 2011

This isn't a particularly "up" story. But cancer isn't a particularly "up" kind of illness. I do my best to cope with it and to lead as normal a life as I can. This blog, this awesome family and friend site (CaringBridge) gives me a chance to talk about how this disease is impacting me every day. I am so sorry when I pour out my soul to this blog, knowing that those that are supporting me are hoping for good reports. It's hard though when some days I can hardly walk because this beast has chewed through the bones in my hip and my spine and my lower back. It takes me two hours or more to be able to get out of bed in the morning, so I set my alarm to 3:00 a.m. in order to take pain medications so that I can get to work by seven just because the pain prevents any meaningful movement. It is devastating to me as I've been working since I was a twelve-year-old boy on a farm, picking potatoes in the muckland in South Lima, hopping out of bed at three to be at work when the sun came up. No, the beast will not end my working days until it ends my life. I promise you, and I promise myself.

It was a rugged autumn for a while. I did a couple of five-day stints in the hospital as the beast gnawed away at the spinal vertebrae, which in turn caused nerve damage. The nerve damage in my pelvis and lower back affected mostly those muscles that control my gastrointestinal and genitourinary control. Things got so backed up that I wound up with urosepsis, a systemic infection that potentially could have spelled my demise. I had a bilateral kidney infection, threatening renal failure. The results of this miserable beast's adventures have been misery for me and a threat to my very existence. Thankfully, the doctors and the hospital have regained the upper hand. And here I am, back at work. I will continue to work.

Pain sits at the top of my everyday concerns, but Morphine and Oxycodone control it for the most part. The most miserable part of the beast's miserable adventure is my inability to control urine flow and, at times, bowels. I have had to have an indwelling catheter since the 23rd of August. Without it, I have constant flow. With it, I can at least function in society with the aid of this tube and bag and adult underwear to keep me on the dry side. I need to stay near a bathroom as I have to empty this infernal bag every half hour or so. I pray daily for the healing of the nerves and the renewed muscle (sphincter control) and the removal of this tube and the bag that hangs from my leg. I wish to die a full man and not as an infant in a diaper. God willing, I will if it is His will.

I know the beast rides within me. A dark shadow accompanies me every day and everywhere I go. I no longer fear the shadow. It is no longer a threat to me. Strangely enough, I have had some very vivid dreams since my urosepsis. Maybe the infection has affected my brain. The dreams come every night. I don't remember all of them, but one stands out this week. I was in a house of some sort. I was trying to paint the rooms in the house. Suddenly there were three of us painting, one in each room. There was a female. I couldn't see her face and she didn't speak, but I felt so comfortable in her presence and so at ease and at peace. She was a wonderful painter and so fast. She painted her room blue with beautiful accessories of many colors and with many colorful lights. The second room was being painted by my brother. I was able to speak to him and he to me. It was my older brother who was killed forty-five years ago in a car accident. He was still sixteen years old, and we poked fun at how each was painting his room. I was having much difficulty in my room. I was trying to paint it yellow, but something kept interfering with me and I couldn't get the color to stick on the wall. I went to see my brother in his room. He had it all done, and it was a beautiful green, but he was gone and didn't answer when I called out to him. Then I went back to the blue room. It too was all done, and the lights and furniture and paintings on the wall were beyond beautiful. They spoke of peace and comfort. I called out to the female to help with my room, but she was gone too and didn't answer me. I suddenly knew who she was as I looked around. It was my mother. She was gone along with my brother. They were both gone and despite the fact that I couldn't finish my yellow room, I felt that it was okay. I woke up quite suddenly after that dream ended. I had no pain and was able to get out of bed without taking a handful of pain medications. I kept going back to that dream all day long. I hoped to return to it the next night, but it just wasn't there. I will remember the green and blue rooms even as I lament that I haven't finished my yellow room. I was so glad that my brother spoke to me that night. I haven't thought very much about him for forty years. I think of mother often and was near tears as I wished I had talked more to her in my dream. It was a dream after all, wasn't it?

There might be some meaning in that dream and the several other dreams that I can't quite recall from the last month or so. I will struggle along with the misery of this awful cancer and the beast that seeks to destroy me. I will continue to work every single day and to stay active and to be a part of my family and my friends. I will try to live as normal a life as I can, for I will not give in to the shadow or the beast until finally, this body cannot function anymore. I promise you. I promise myself. I promise my God.

February 10th, 2012

Two thousand twelve has been hard. I spent a good part of January in hospital as this awful beast goes about its awful task. I had an MRI this week and had the opportunity to look at it closely. I saw the beast and the work it's done. It has ravaged my spinal vertebrae, my pelvis, both in the sacrum and the pelvic wings. It's left terrible lesions and growths which cause unbelievable pain. They are in my back, pelvis, hip, femur, and tibia. Now a tumor in my hip joint along with three fractures of my hip due to the weakened bone have made it a true challenge to be able to walk, stand up and sit. The pain is excruciating and laid me out flat in my bed (or the hospital's bed) for two full weeks. Lying flat is the only thing that gives me any kind of relief.

The beast has ruined my body but not my spirit. The beast has managed to overcome me with agony and pain, but it has not overcome my faith. The beast has caused me to use up every penny of my life savings to the point where it has become difficult to even make my co-pays to get medical help. Even though it has just about ruined me financially, it has not been able to ruin my family or my friendships. I will continue to fight this battle. I may do it from a hospital bed, but I won't give it up. I'm free of the hospital for now, thanks to some pretty powerful pain killers. Even those may wind up, costing me my job if the beast manages to damage me so badly that I can no longer walk or sit. I'm not going to make it easy for the beast though. I promise to live. I promise to fight back.

I believe in angels and the work they do in the name of God. The angels surround me. They keep that terrible shadow away from me. The comfort that knowledge brings to me, especially knowing that there is a purpose in all of this, keeps me sane and hopeful.

I begin chemo treatments again this coming week. Radiation is ahead of me after that. I will survive that. I will survive the financial difficulties. I will survive the limited mobility. I will survive the pain. I will live life despite this beast. I have my family. I have some pretty amazing friends and friendships. I have my faith. With all of this, how could I not survive?

It has been a month of pain and tears, of worry and illness, but it has also been a month of love, support and comfort as those that love me have proven love over and over. They have been at my side this whole month. They have not abandoned me. I could not live if they did abandon me. So, I am alive. I continue to be alive because of that love and support. I will not let those that love me down. I will be worthy of that love and support. I am so thankful for what I have. I am so thankful for you.

February 17th, 2012

I received some positive news from the doctors this week. It was the first bright spot for me in a month of pain and blue days. I'm sorry to expose my friends and loved ones to my depression last week. It's just that some days, things seem so bleak, and the tears are overwhelming. I pour out my heart to this diary, not to scare you or make you feel sorry for me but because I am looking for support and know I can find it in you. I believe that this beast is trying to terrorize me. I may not be responsible for getting knocked down by this beast, but I'm certainly responsible for getting back up. So here I am today, back up. We can throw stones, complain about them, stumble on them, climb over them, or build with them. I choose to climb over them and use them to build a more positive future.

I know that you've stood by me in my blue times. I remember now that the person who thinks about his own grief forgets about the grief of others. I know that I'm not the sickest person in the world and that there are many others who suffer far more than I do. I refuse to forget the pain and grief of others and promise myself to think about them first and do everything I can to help others and build them up. And when I find that I'm lying flat in the hospital bed because the beast has knocked me down, I keep in mind that occasional failure in this battle is only a detour, it's not a dead-end street.

I'm back on some chemo now and a new medication, which is most promising. I was up against a brick wall last week and found out that I don't have to be stopped by it but that I can go over it or around it. That's where I'm going. Carpe diem!

March 23rd, 2012

I walked outside in the predawn this morning. There was a heavy dew and the air was fresh and clean. The birds were chattering, and I could just see the first rays of the rising sun on the eastern horizon. I took a deep breath and thought to myself, "How could this be other than a wonderful day to be alive?"

I spent a couple of weeks in hospital and have been out and back to work for a week now. I visit with my doctors regularly, and they tell me I am holding my own. My wife may not have thought so two weeks ago when she came downstairs early in the morning and found me unconscious on the dining room floor. The ambulance came—what an incredible group of professionals they are! In short order, I arrived in the emergency room at Clifton Springs Hospital. I was diagnosed with a massive blood infection and septic shock. They suspect that I suffered another TIA.

I've been up and about now for over a week and feeling rather healthy. Where the beast has caused much damage, the surgeons will now go in and repair. The "fix" should help to prevent further massive infections and allow me a more stable and normal life. It is major surgery to implant an artificial urinary sphincter. The beast destroyed my own. The surgery will take place on May 10th at Highland Hospital. I'm told that the surgeon performing the procedure is the very best in the field. Although I'm not looking forward to the six weeks of recovery and the pain of the surgery, I welcome the chance to strike back at the beast and to say to it, "You haven't won yet!"

My beautiful wife and I are going to visit my brother and his children and grandchildren in San Diego at the end of April. I am looking forward to that distraction with great joy and anticipation. When I return, the great fight is on.

A good part of 2011 was spent in the hospital and home, recovering from my various battles with the beast. I am now looking forward to a peaceful and healthier 2012 as we seek to drive the beast back. God is with me. He has sent His angels to guard me and to guide the hands of the doctors. How can I fail? I will go outside my house daily and thank my God for his care of me. I will breathe the fresh spring air and listen to the birds sing to each other. I will know the beauty of life and thank God for the opportunity to enjoy it every day just as I did this morning.

April 16th, 2012

I have passed the three-year mark. Three years ago this month, the physicians just gave me three years. Actually I'm feeling pretty good right now and think that I most likely have another three years with little trouble, except that I recently fell and broke my leg. Things like falling and breaking legs do not lend themselves to long life.

It amazes me every single day how many good, generous and thoughtful people there are in this world. As I move about on crutches or with a cane or in a wheelchair, I've discovered that the nightly news and the newspapers have a very narrow vision of the real world. Don't get me wrong, there's a lot of nasty stuff going on out there (and definitely some nasty people); but by and large, humans are good and decent, thoughtful and compassionate. I could cite numerous little events where complete strangers have gone out of their way to assist me in public places, stores, parking lots, at doorways and just walking with my assist devices.

This whole affair set me to thinking about myself and my own virtues. It really comes down to about a dozen that really make a difference. If it makes me a better person to my brethren, doesn't it make a better world overall?

I'm not a big churchgoer. Don't get me wrong, I do go to church occasionally and enjoy the fellowship, but I have a close relationship with God on my own. I believe, despite all the religions in the world, that there is but one God who made all things. I believe that it is important to worship God by adoration and thanksgiving for all that is good and right and beautiful in this world. I believe that my soul is immortal. I believe that the most acceptable service of God is doing good to man. I believe that God will absolutely reward virtue and punish vice, either here or hereafter.

What has befallen me in regard to events in my life and my health is what it is. To an extent, I can influence it, especially if I choose a selfish and self-serving path through life. If on the other hand I choose to think about my life in terms of the dozen or so virtues, then I hope that I might have a bit of that reward when finally I move into the hereafter.

With all of that said, these are what I believe are virtues to live by to which I commit myself, some suggested by Benjamin Franklin in his various writings:

Temperance—I eat not to overfill nor drink to drunkenness.

Thoughtful silence—I speak only that which will benefit others and, when speaking, do so with an open mind, knowing that I could be wrong and another person right.

Order—I keep myself and my home and business out of confusion.

Resolution—I resolve to perform what I should and perform without fail what I have resolved and promised to do.

Frugality—I take care of money and values by wasting nothing at all.

Industrious time—Always be employed in something useful, enlightening, and educational.

Sincerity—I never deceive. I think justly. And when I speak, I speak according to my beliefs but with an open mind.

Justice—Do no injury to any person on this earth, ever. That includes treating every person with respect no matter their situation in life.

Moderation—Avoid extremes.

Cleanliness—I will tolerate no uncleanliness to body, mind, or habitation.

Tranquility—I refuse to be disturbed by trifles and especially rumor.

Humility—I will imitate Jesus and Socrates.

I'm looking forward to many years yet. I'm not going down so easily as the doctors would suggest. Knowing and living the virtues I've mentioned will bring me rewards here and in the hereafter.

June 29th, 2012

As I make my way through this challenge to my health and my life, I've had wonderful experiences and suffered through many dark days. It's also taught me to notice the people around me—no, not so much to notice but instead to pay attention. As bad as I sometimes feel, as dark as it often looks, I see others who suffer more. Believe it or not, often it's not the "patient" who suffers so much as the people who love the patient. Their anguish has been hard for me to watch as I go through radiation and chemo, seeing them sitting quietly in the waiting rooms, sometimes talking quietly with others, sometimes sobbing in their despair. I like to believe that when we lose someone close to us, they still live through us. The time we have spent with those we've lost makes them part of us, and through those memories, they live the life we are each living every day. Because of our love and those memories, they live on.

I came through my recent surgery very nicely. The results have me flying high; I'm on cloud nine. The infections are all resolved and haven't recurred. The catheters and bags are gone. The wet diapers that I've lived in for the last ten months are gone. I feel as though I've been released from a dark, damp prison and I'm free again, renewed, refreshed.

I've just finished the latest round of radiation aimed at resolving the tremendous pain in my back and pelvis. I've developed severe swelling in my left leg, making it difficult to walk comfortably and, at times, almost impossible to get my shoe on. What can one do? Go barefoot. There's always a way out, an answer.

I continue to go to work every day. I'm supposed to work no more than three hours per day. I really enjoy the challenges I'm faced with at work. It keeps me focused and believing that I can continue to accomplish important work. It's not easy sometimes. I wake up usually around 3:00 a.m. and begin taking pain medications just so that I can get up, walk, and function. Usually by 5:00 or 6:00 a.m., I can make it through a shower and get in the car to drive to work. The doctors have doubled my pain medication and that has helped. Although I think it's affecting my memory and ability to think quickly. I lose track of words and thoughts easily and struggle through conversations and meetings. Most people are patient. Most understand. I will undergo a bone scan, CT and MRI and some x-rays over the next couple of weeks as we seek out the whereabouts of this beast and its tentacles and to push back, to fight back.

You know, in the end, we rely upon each other to get through our troubles. The friendships I've made and the people who have expressed and given me support for the last three years will be a treasure to me for however many months and years I may have left. I hope that through my experiences, I will be able to help and support others who are worse off than I am. Maybe then, when it's my time to leave this world, I will be able to live on through someone's love and memory of me. We never die when we love.

October 31st, 2012

I haven't been here in a while. It's been a long few months and a period of pain and depression. I write this as I return from a Caribbean cruise, a short respite from this nightmare. I'm sitting here feeling the spray of ocean on my bare chest and face at 5:00 a.m. as I make my way home from a cruise to eastern Caribbean Islands, a very restful and refreshing vacation. I'm feeling depressed and anxious. This body is giving host to the terrible beast who is doing its upmost to break my spirit and my faith through intense and unrelenting pain. I am taking a multitude of "pills". These pills have themselves changed my health. They constipate, make dizzy, cause nausea, fatigue and a plethora of other miseries. I've gained weight, which I can't seem to lose. I'm bloated and I feel miserable with just a mouthful of food.

Old and dear friends speak kindly to me with great compassion and empathy, but I'm no longer invited to participate in activities, even lunch and such simple things with them that I once did with regularity and joy. I'm certain it's a result of concern on their part for my strength and physical pain and worry for my health. It saddens me beyond comprehension. That's why I sit here and feel the sea, listening to the waves in the early morning darkness and think how inviting that darkness is. How easy it would be to fling this wrecked body over the rail and join the peace and tranquility of the universe.

I've seen the beast this week. It is a large tumor, which has sprung from my thoracic vertebrae and taken the place of the vertebral bone on T4, T5, T6, T7, T8, and T9. The tumor impinged upon my thoracic aorta by about 20 percent, causing chest pain, shortness of breath and blood pressure problems. I have intense pain in my right flank. The tumor has wrapped around my spinal cord and sent its tentacles through the neural foramens of T7–T8, and T9, compressing my spinal cord and nerves exiting, threatening to paralyze me from the waist down. I've started a fourteen-day round of emergent and intense radiotherapy in an effort to thwart the beast and shrink the tumor. Next will be chemo to kill off any remaining cancer cells from the tumor and hope that the microscopic cells haven't escaped into my cerebral spinal fluid and traveled to my brain only to create more tumors there. The beast is on an all-out attack now. I looked at my MRI and have seen my enemy. I fear the unknown but don't fear what I can see. I am ready to fight. Bring it on. This beast is slowly getting the upper hand. The shadow, which has been in my constant presence for almost two years, grows darker and colder. I think its name is death and it waits to carry me away to the ages. We'll see. October is upon me. Oblivion is not far off.

Please stay near me, dear friend, you are my support and my hope.

November 7th, 2012

A wave of sadness washed over me this morning. My heart was weeping as I drove back to my ambulance base. I had opportunity to drive a young paramedic student from my base to his assigned ambulance crew. We had a very nice talk. He's in his second year in emergency medical services and was headed out to do some field clinical work as he strives to obtain his paramedic certification. We talked about my years in EMS, in the field, in the military, in the classroom, and as administrator for my ambulance company. I dropped him off and wished him well and saw myself in him almost forty years ago.

As I returned toward my base, I had occasion go to the local hospital because three of our ambulances were headed there with patients from various parts or our county. I was able to meet them as they came in. I was able to assist them unloading patients and wheel those patients to triage. I had a chance to say hi to each of the five patients being brought in by our crews. I asked them how they were doing and if their trip was comfortable. Each one of them told me how nice our crews were, how compassionate and empathetic as well as professional, how those paramedics made a difference on their bad day.

As I came into the emergency room, I saw a couple of nurses and a doctor there that I've worked with for years. They greeted me as though I still worked the streets every day, and they were genuine. They were acknowledged colleagues who shook my hand and said it was so great to see me in the lineup again.

I left the emergency room with this feeling of deep sadness. How much doing this thing meant to me: emergency care of sick and injured, scared and uncertain patients and how I knew I could help them and how often I have done just that. Now this beast has taken that from me and I can only stand on the side and watch others do the things that I love to do. I have given almost two-thirds of my entire life to ministering to mankind in an effort to leave earth in a better condition than I found it. I did that daily for a good part of my life and it was and is possible the most rewarding thing I could ever have done.

I believe in angels and the work they do in God's name for the benefit of mankind. I live with a deep and abiding faith in the design of a higher intelligence and believe that I had a part in the destiny of man and for its betterment. I am so devastated that my time for that ministry may be at an end and I don't have a clear understanding of why. I will maintain my faith and hold back the weeping heart, control my sadness at my inability to continue what I so love in the hopes that there is yet more for me to do and that the beast hasn't won in this so important reason for my life.

April 2nd, 2013

Does death terrify you? It doesn't me. Yet as I sit in the oncologist's office, I watch the patients come and go and I see that fear of death. I also see sadness and a certain dread. Perhaps it is the dread of the unpleasant treatment they are about to receive, and perhaps it is knowing, for many, that it isn't going to make any difference in the outcome.

Death is coming to all of us. It might be this cancer, a car accident, the result of this angry and violent world, or any number of diseases that mankind still seeks to overcome. Death is with me. It is a shadow that follows me. It's not threatening, but it's there. I can feel it. Sometimes it's right next to me, other times it just seems to follow me. Sometimes I can see it like a dark shadow off in the corner of the room. I don't think it wants to take me away, but I think it knows my fate. It knows that the time is coming closer. When this awful beast, that is cancer, has torn up enough of this poor body, then finally death will touch me and help me to leave this world.

Death isn't a vengeful creature; it doesn't seek to consume me the way the beast does, but instead it is a conductor from the world we all know into yet another existence. I love this world and all the people that I know and love that are on this ride with me that we call life. I don't want to leave that behind. I know that love. I'm comfortable in my world as it is. When I have to give in to this beast, then I will go with death into an unknown world, another existence. It excites me as well as saddens me, but it doesn't scare me. If we all are destined to go with death into the next existence, then I am certain that those that I love and cherish will at some point be in my new existence.

So as the beast continues to tear this body apart and cause me ever-increasing pain, I will refuse to give up. Nope, the beast can't just have this body, so I'll struggle to keep it for myself and my loved ones and suffer whatever the beast causes me to suffer until at last I don't have the strength left to continue the fight. I'm not afraid. Just a little sad at all that must stay behind until once again, those that I love will come together with me again. It will be okay. It will be fine.

July 10th, 2013

It has been quite a while since I last made an entry into this journal. It's not because of any great change in my health (although there have been some significant changes) but more because I'm just out of energy. It has become an effort to just sit up in bed in the morning. It often takes me over an hour to get up, take the appropriate medication and then force myself to get moving.

I had surgery on my back on May 23rd to remove cancerous vertebrae in my lumbar spine and then place a wire and strap metal device and fuse both sections into a usable back. It's been a tough go of it. On top of all of that, I was hospitalized for osteomyelitis, bacteremia, DVTs in both legs and a PE, along with various other complications. It seems like we get one problem cleared up and then another takes its place. I was hospitalized last week for a serious infection in my left foot and leg, which was spreading so fast you could almost watch it climb up my leg. No time to rest and recuperate from problem one before we are treating problem two or three or four. It's never-ending, so it seems, and its energy is sapping.

But in the end, I am still breathing, walking (short distances—stairs are a nightmare). You know, as tough as it is, it's still a pleasure to wake up and feel the fresh morning breeze on my face in the morning, to see the sunshine, and hear the birds sing. There are times when I honestly think that I'm not going to be able to draw my next breath and then I hear the calls of the newborn bird chicks—what a thrill. I know that I can get up and get going, and so I sit up (screams and moans are optional) and slowly but surely up, up and away.

The two eleven-year-old boys from Ireland arrived last Friday night. They are great kids, but wow—I forgot how much work it is to keep up and it's just incredible the energy that they have. I'm hoping to tap into that energy reserve. First I have to catch them!

Carpe diem, my dear friends. I am aiming for the end of the year, but it's going to be an uphill battle, I fear.

August 9th, 2013

Tonight, August 8th, one of my dearest and most loyal friends died in my arms. For fourteen and a half years, he came running to me as I walked through the door every single time. He greeted me with a big smile and a wagging tail. He knew how my day went as soon as I reached down to acknowledge and pet him. If I was having a good day, he danced around my legs and begged to be lifted up so that he could kiss my face and share in my sunshine. If I was having a bad day, it didn't change his approach, but he was more subdued. He would come and sit next to me quietly and just stare out from his perch, daring anyone to interrupt my thoughts until I started to feel better. For a little guy, he made a fearsome guard.

It didn't matter what went on in my life, he was tuned in and gave me his rapt attention and understanding. At the end, as he grew older, especially over the last month or so, his age slowed him down (all except for that energetic wagging tail). He had heart failure, arthritis. He was mostly blind and truly hard of hearing. He always amazed me because despite his blindness and hearing problems, he always seemed to know it was me at the backdoor. And as painful as it must have been, he continued to hurry across the dining room to greet me.

When I got home last night, he came running out to greet me and then just sat down as if to say, "Boss, I'm out of gas". Poko laid on his side and just worked to breathe. I said to my wife, "He is dying. I don't think he'll be here much more than a few hours". I sat on the floor next to him, holding him and stroking his head. Within twenty minutes, he had a short hypoxic seizure and then quietly went to sleep. Forever.

I don't mind admitting that I held him and cried for an hour. God, this hurts so much.

After I buried him (with the help of my brother), I spent a good part of the night just thinking about Poko and the friendship we shared for going on fifteen years. Then I realized what a lesson that awesome little dog has given me. That no matter how I feel, I have to be cognizant of the feelings and moods and troubles of those around me. Despite any pain and fatigue that I might be having, like my black moods and bad health days, I have to look at others around me and give them the value of my friendship and caring like the brotherhood of the "boss and his dog", to greet others with the proverbial tail wagging and sometimes give them a huge smile and a big hug, dancing around and enjoying the good day they might be having. On those days where my friend might be feeling low or having pain and suffering, maybe just acknowledge that and sit quietly by just listening or just being next to them.

That's the lesson I learned from Poko's life and from his death. May I be as loyal to my friends and brethren and as empathetic to their suffering or their happiness as Poko was for mine. I will always miss my friend and I will always remember the lessons he gave me in his life and in his death.

God, may I live up to his example and I pray that I might be such an example to my fellow man as I approach my final days, hours, and minutes.

*****

This was the last entry into Ken's online journal. Ken was to survive the dreaded October month, which his father, brother and mother all passed away in. He was able to spend the holidays with friends and family. February 7th, 2014, Ken was admitted to the hospital for his pain, at this moment, Ken made it aware to family and friends that he was ready, he was done fighting and wanted the pain to end. Sunday, February 9th, the doctors made it aware that Ken had days left to live.

Ken entered into eternity on March 9, 2014, at the Hospeace House in Naples.

Ken, we will strive to "Carpe diem" for you. We will strive to "Seize the day!"

Kenneth W. Kelly's obituary from Fuller Home, Inc.

Canandaigua, New York—Ken Kelly, 62, of Chapin Street passed away March 9th, 2014, at Hospeace House in Naples after a long battle with cancer.

Ken was predeceased by his beloved mother, Gloria; father, Fred; brother, Fred; and animal companion, Poko.

He is survived by his wife, Mary "Mickie" Kelly; brothers, Al Kelly, Ed (Kathy) Kelly, Scott (Tracey) Kelly, David (Kathy) Kelly; stepchildren, Jamie (Amy) Alexander, William (Ann Marie) Alexander, Aaron Alexander; step-grandchildren; several nieces and nephews; and many dear friends including, Dylan, John, Lisa and Treff.

Ken loved family, friends, life, the beach, his career, and people. He lived by the motto, "Carpe diem" and often was heard exclaiming, "It is what it is".

He was the Chief Operating Officer and General Manager of Finger Lakes Ambulance from 1993–2013.

Ken was the founder and instructor of the EMT/Paramedic program at FLCC from 1997–2008. He was awarded the New York State Emergency Medical Services Educator of Excellence Award on Saturday, October 17th, 2009.

Friends may call Friday, March 14th, from 3:00–4:00 and 7:00–9:00 p.m. at Fuller Funeral Home, Inc., 190 Buffalo Street, Canandaigua. An 11:00 a.m. funeral service will be held Saturday, March 15th, at Crosswinds Church, 3360 Middle Cheshire Road, Canandaigua. Burial will be in Oak Ridge Cemetery.

In lieu of flowers, please make a contribution to one of the following: Hospeace House, Inc., PO Box 343 Naples, New York 14512, Finger Lakes Ambulance, www.fingerlakesambulance.com, Clifton Springs Fire Department, www.cliftonspringsfd.org or the American Cancer society, 1120 Goodman Street, Rochester, New York 14620.

EMS leader made world a little better (from the Finger Lakes Times by Julie Sherwood)

Canandaigua—It isn't often that one person during his or her lifetime is able to touch the lives of hundreds of others—in ways that heal and teach life lessons.

Ken Kelly was one of those people, say his many friends and family.

"He made lives better. He gave and gave without wanting recognition. He was a teacher, a boss and a friend," said John Years, one of those mourning the loss of Mr. Kelly, who died March 9th, 2014, at the age of sixty-two.

A Paramedic and Paramedic Instructor, Mr. Kelly was longtime Chief Operation Officer and General Manager of Finger

Lakes Ambulance. He was also a founder of the Emergency Medical Technician/Paramedics program at Finger Lakes Community College and the program's instructor for nearly ten years until 2008. He also helped develop a full-time Advanced Life Support program for Finger Lakes Ambulance, the first paramedic level ALS in a four-county area of the Finger Lakes.

After Army service as a Military Police Officer, Mr. Kelly returned to the Finger Lakes region and continued his service as an Emergency Medical Technician, rising through the ranks and working with multiple agencies, including Canandaigua Ambulance, Victor Farmington Ambulance, Ontario County Advanced Life Support, and then Finger Lakes Ambulance.

Paul Hood, a friend and former student, in a tribute to Mr. Kelly on the Heroes Memorial Foundation Page (http://heroesmemorial.org/), recounted that Mr. Kelly "quickly realized that there was a large need for a paramedic instructor in the region. So after taking the course in Syracuse, he set out to bring the program to the area. His actions enabled a whole new class of people to undertake the training locally and to be some of the best paramedics in the state," Hood wrote.

"Ken enjoyed life," Hood added, stating Mr. Kelly "believed that it was our responsibility to make the world a little better than we found it. As an instructor, his students went on to be Army Medics in Iraq and other theaters of operations throughout the world. His students have risen to leadership roles in Emergency Medical Services, and they continue to teach in the same manner that they were taught."

"Mr. Kelly took students under his wing and taught not only the necessary skills but educated through example about morals and dealing with all kinds of life situations," said Years.

He said he met Mr. Kelly as a teenager while working for him years ago when Mr. Kelly was a manager at West's Shurfine Food Market in Honeoye. They quickly became friends, said Years, adding that bond grew to become like family and carried on to the next generation. He said Mr. Kelly became a beloved "uncle" to his son, Dylan.

"Mr. Kelly enjoyed the outdoors, sports, and camaraderie with a wide circle of friends and family," said Years.

"He always paid it forward and put everyone ahead of himself," he said.

"He was a great inspiration, a great teacher and mentor, and he took care of his family," said Mr. Kelly's brother, Ed Kelly. One of many examples is when after their father died, Ed said Ken became the family's father figure, filling a void with his leadership and compassion.

Mr. Kelly's wife, Mary "Mickie" Kelly, said she and Ken met some twenty years ago at Finger Lakes Ambulance.

"He wanted to make it his career and I wanted to make it mine too," she recalled.

They became good friends, a relationship that grew but remained simply a friendship for nearly ten years until after one night when Mr. Kelly invited her over for a family dinner. Mickie kept the love letter Ken wrote to her not long after, expressing his feelings for her. They were married August 28th, 2004. He was a loving husband, Mickie said, recalling that early on, she knew Ken was special and that there was no one else she would rather be with.

At Finger Lakes Ambulance, Mr. Kelly's successor, Director of Operations, Bill Comella, said Ken left "some huge shoes" to fill. Comella, who had worked under Mr. Kelly since 2003, said he admired his leadership skills.

"Ken understood people and how to make them feel like they were part of a team," Comella said. "He was able to bring out the best in each of the people who worked with him. Ken would push you to give more than 100 percent. Ken embodied the idea of staying focused and never giving up right through the end of his life. He has taught me life lessons that will stay with me forever."

About the Author

Ken Kelly had been in Emergency Medical Services since his time as a soldier. He began as an Emergency Medical Technician and worked his career up to be a Paramedic and a Paramedic Instructor and so very much more.

Mickie Kelly became a Licensed Practical Nurse in 1968 and an EMT volunteer in 1988.

Ken began at Finger Lakes Ambulance in Clifton Springs, New York, in late 1993, and Mickie started there in March of 1994 as an EMT/Dispatcher.

Ken and Mickie met, worked together and became friends. That is a love story in itself, and they were married on August 28, 2004.

Ken began his greatest challenge on April 20th, 2009, until his passing on March 9th, 2014.

Mickie continues to be a volunteer EMT and an EMS Captain for Hopewell Fire Department, just east of Canandaigua, New York. She has learned so very much from this amazing man and will continue to pass on the legacy of his teachings, inspiring thoughts, insights and so very much more.

CPSIA information can be obtained
at www.ICGtesting.com
Printed in the USA
BVHW020052210122
625948BV00005B/20